Make a Mil-¥en

Make a Mil-¥en

Teaching English in Japan

DON BEST

STONE BRIDGE PRESS
Berkeley, California

Material on page 81 from *Dave Barry Does Japan* used by permission (© Dave Barry 1992).

Published by STONE BRIDGE PRESS
P.O. Box 8208
Berkeley, California 94707
TEL 510-524-8732
FAX 510-524-8711

10 9 8 7 6 5 4 3 2 1

Printed in the United States of America.

Library of Congress Cataloging-in-Publication Data

Best, Don.
Make a mil-yen : teaching English in Japan / Don Best.
p. cm.
Includes index.
ISBN 1-880656-11-6.
1. English philology—Study and teaching—Japan—Vocational guidance. 2. English language—Study and teaching—Japanese speakers—Vocational guidance. 3. English teachers—Employment—Japan. 4. Americans—Employment—Japan. I. Title.
PE68.J3B47 1994
428'.0023'52—dc20 93-44380
CIP

Contents

Introduction

You really can make a million teaching English conversation in Japan. I made over ¥7 million during the 18 months I taught in Japan. That comes out to well over $50,000, and $20,000 of that came home with me in the form of savings.

I didn't go to Japan for the money. I had hit my late twenties' crisis, the "What-the-hell-am-I-going-to-do-with-the-rest-of-my-life" phase, and wanted a little adventure. I had heard that there were lots of jobs available teaching English in Japan, and that teaching experience and the ability to speak Japanese were not requirements (I didn't have either). This seemed like the perfect chance to have a bit of an adventure, and to at least break even financially (I had no idea I would come back with so much money). So in October 1990, I left my job in California, read two books about Japan, packed much too much luggage and took off.

As soon as I got off the airplane, I realized I didn't have a clue as to what I was doing. I said the wrong thing to the immigration officer, didn't know how to get to Tokyo from the airport and paid a fortune for my room that first night. My ignorance continued to make life interesting through the next few weeks while I searched for a job. Nothing catastrophic happened, but in many situations if I had only had a little forewarning, I could have saved a lot of time, money and frustration. What I really needed was a friend who had been there before to tell me all the secrets and to give me suggestions on how to make my adventure in Japan go a little more smoothly.

That is why I wrote *Make a Mil-¥en,* so that you could benefit from my experience and that of dozens of others who have successfully landed jobs teaching English conversation in Japan.

Make a Mil-¥en is an easy-to-read, beginning-to-end guide to what you need to do to get a job teaching English conversation in Japan. Whether you are an English as a Second Language (ESL) professional, or have no teaching experience, this book answers all of your questions about teaching English in Japan. Although ESL teachers have the obvious qualifications to teach English in Japan, there is room and a need for the non-ESL professional as well. I was not an ESL teacher when I went to Japan and found that it was not a disadvantage as I looked for and found a job. I do recommend that those without ESL training get some experience before they begin their job search, and this book tells you how to do that. One chapter gives advice on how to prepare and execute a demonstration lesson (which could be part of the interview), but this is not a "How to teach English in Japan" book (such books do exist and I tell you what they are). This is a "How to get a *job* teaching English in Japan" book.

Make a Mil-¥en tells you how to prepare for this adventure—a crucial step that I overlooked on my first trip—from what to pack to deciding when to arrive in Japan, plus a lot of things you haven't even thought of. *Make a Mil-¥en* provides insiders' tips about surviving cheaply in Japan until you get your first paycheck. It tells you where to look for jobs, both within Japan and before you leave home. You'll learn how to interview for a job and how to evaluate a potential employer to get the best deal for yourself. *Make a Mil-¥en* even provides some handy information for settling in after you are employed in Japan.

As of December 1993 the job market for English teachers in Japan is probably the toughest it has ever been. The two positive points are that those who are better prepared are getting the jobs now, and as the Japanese economy improves so will the job market for English teachers. Everyone agrees, the need for English teachers in Japan will not go away.

Although the competition has increased, there are still plenty of teaching jobs in Japan. The money's good and the chance for a wonderful experience is just across the Pacific. But unlike my first experience in Japan, you have a friend who can fill you in on all the details–*Make a Mil-¥en.*

Gambatte!

Acknowledgments

This book would not have been possible without the hundreds of Japanese students I had the pleasure to teach and the millions of others in Japan who truly want to learn English so that they can learn more about the world. Thanks to all of my students and in particular the Takano and Okamoto families, my friends Toshi, Yuko and the Boss for making me feel welcome and teaching me about their country.

Besides my personal experience, the primary source of information for this book was my fellow teachers. They provided invaluable advice and assistance to this stranger who entered their community without a clue. With only a hundred of us *gaijin* living in a city of one million people we became a family. Thanks to Paul, Teresa, Brian, Big Red and Colin.

While writing this book it was a pleasure to spend quite a bit of time at the incredibly beautiful and peaceful Green Apple Inn Bed and Breakfast in Sonoma County, California. The hospitality and editorial suggestions of innkeepers Rogers and Rosemary Hoffman were much appreciated. I recommend the Green Apple as a great way to re-enter "reality" after your stay in Japan.

Finally without the support of my entire family my adventure in Japan and the writing of this book would not have been as successful as they were. Thanks to my sister-in-law Keiko for her expertise on Japan, to my father, Bob Best, for his logical and creative contributions and to my mother, Marge Best, who deserves more credit (and money) than I can provide here for lending her professional writing and editing expertise (and a great deal of patience) to the production of this book. Thank you.

1

The Most Common Questions

The Basics of Teaching English in Japan

Don't I have to speak Japanese?
Shouldn't I be an expert in English grammar?
Don't I need a teaching credential?

No is the answer to all of these questions. I wish I had a hundred yen for everybody who believes that speaking Japanese, being an expert in English grammar and having teaching experience are all necessary to make money teaching English in Japan. They are not.

Unfortunately I don't get the yen, and the people who believe that the above are prerequisites miss out on a wonderful opportunity (and millions of yen). You'll see why the above aren't necessary and learn more about teaching English in Japan as I answer more of the most common questions.

How Can I Teach If I Don't Speak Japanese?

The fact is, you don't need to speak a word of Japanese to teach English conversation in Japan. The main reason is that all Japanese students study English for six years in junior and senior high schools. The problem for the Japanese students is that they only study English in written form; they rarely if ever speak it. Consequently, they have a lot of English knowledge in their heads (they probably know more English grammar than the average American), but they can't get it to come out of their mouths in an intelligible manner.

This is where you, the person with native English-speaking ability, comes in. Every year over nine million Japanese of all ages seek help in improving their English conversation skills. They all need a teacher to help them. The only skill most language schools require of their teachers is native English-speaking ability. You qualify!

How Do You Teach English Conversation?

Teaching English conversation is simply teaching communication skills. In most cases this means providing your students with words or phrases and then practicing with them. It does not generally include the grammar and punctuation that your high school English teacher tried to drill into your head (out of respect to my high school English teacher and my aunt, a retired English teacher, I always referred to myself as a teacher of English communication skills—not as an English teacher).

Can I Teach Without Any Experience?

Yes, you can. Most foreigners who teach English conversation in Japan's language schools started with little or no teaching experience, and it still isn't usually a requirement today. The language school that hires you will teach you everything it thinks you need to know to be a successful teacher.

Having some kind of teaching experience, however, will be an asset when you look for a teaching job in Japan. If you don't think you have relevant experience, see Chapter 3, "Qualifications and Experience." You may have developed teaching skills and experience without realizing it. You will also learn how to gain some formal teaching experience before you leave for Japan.

A formal education in teaching, or actual teaching experience, opens up a few more possibilities. The more prestigious and higher paying positions at universities are open to those who have a Master of Arts or certificate in Teaching English as a Second Language (TESL).

Even if you don't have teaching experience, you still have the most important qualification: You are a native speaker of English.

Who Can Teach English in Japan?

Anybody who has native English-speaking ability can teach English in Japan, but a university degree is usually required for most teaching positions. It is possible to work legally without a university degree, if you obtain a cultural visa. The cultural visa is explained on page 128.

Men and women of all ages and ethnic backgrounds are teaching English in Japan today. I met *sensei* (sen-say: a term of respect used for teachers; also used for doctors and lawyers) of all ages, from the recent college grad to those 50 and older. A few schools still like to recruit *sensei* under the age of 35, but this is not true of all schools. The average age of the 10 teachers at the language school I worked for was 36; the youngest was 24 and the oldest 51.

In the past it was thought that language schools in Japan hired only blue-eyed blondes. Today, however, the Japanese are becoming much more sensitive to diversity, and men and women of many ethnic backgrounds with native English ability are employed as teachers. I have friends of Chinese, African and Latin descent who are currently teaching English in Japan. Asians might have some difficulty being accepted as English conversation *sensei* because the Japanese don't expect them to be fluent in English; but as evidenced by my Chinese friend, this prejudice can be overcome.

Why the Big Demand for English Teachers?

This question could be reworded as: *Why are Japanese so obsessed with learning English?* For they truly are. To begin with, Japan is an economic world power and English is the international business language. Having practically no natural resources, Japan's prosperity is completely dependent on international markets. The Japanese know that the ability to communicate in English is an essential business tool; to be successful they must speak English. Japanese companies account for most of the money spent on English conversation by providing lessons for their *sarariman* (sa-ra-ree-man: Japanese male office worker), who study at their workplace.

The Japanese government also knows that learning English is important. To increase the nation's awareness of its emerging role in the global community (particularly in the business scene), the government has been conducting an "Internationalization" campaign since the 1980s. The goal is to make the people of this historically isolated island nation more aware of the outside world and the people of the world more familiar with Japan.

In an informal poll I asked hundreds of Japanese: *What does Internationalization mean to you?* The usual answer was: *Learning English.* In effect, learning English is a national campaign. This is further evidenced by the six-year English study requirement in school and the importance of the English test on the killer college entrance exams (literally; some Japanese students have committed suicide after failing the exams).

This is why millions of Japanese are continually trying to improve their English conversation skills in traditional schools and at over 8,000 English conversation language schools throughout the country. All of these institutions need native English speakers, and since most foreigners who teach English conversation stay only a year or two, there are constant openings.

How Much Can I Make Teaching in Japan?

This is a very important (if not the most important) question for anyone considering teaching in Japan. The Japanese Ministry of Justice's Immigration Division has issued guidelines stating that foreigners engaged in the instruction of language (English teachers) should receive a guaranteed monthly salary of at least ¥250,000 ($2,273).* The Japanese government also recommends that foreign instructors of language receive company-paid health care and apartment assistance.

It's important to note that this salary is usually based on teaching only 20 to 30 hours a week, depending on the school. You should receive additional pay at a higher rate for any hours you work over the specified minimum.

---

*When I specify an amount of money in yen, I include a dollar amount parenthetically, based on an exchange rate of ¥110 yen to $1 U.S. The exchange rate will vary. Check the business section of your newspaper for the current exchange rate.

The big money comes during those hours you teach after your required minimum teaching hours. You can earn from ¥3,000 ($27) to as much as ¥10,000 ($91) an hour teaching overtime for your school, part-time for another school or private lessons.

With a little effort, working some overtime and being a thrifty consumer, you should easily be able to save at least $500/month (see sample budget on the next page). Teachers who really hustle (work over 40 hours/week) can save as much, or more than, $2,000/month. A good friend of mine, a 40-year-old Australian who has taught in Japan for three years, was saving between $2,500 and $3,000 a month as recently as March 1993.

Chapter 10, "Compensation," provides greater detail on salaries. You will find more information on part-time work and private lessons on page 136.

The direction of the exchange rate can have either a negative or positive effect on you, both as a tourist (before you find a job) and as a teacher receiving a paycheck. As a tourist you want your dollar to buy as many yen as possible, so the higher the yen to the dollar the better. As an income earner you want to use as few yen as possible to buy a dollar. I was unlucky when I went to Japan because as a job seeker I could only buy about ¥125 with $1, but when I began receiving a paycheck the exchange rate changed and it took around ¥140 to buy a $1. I know this gets confusing but you will catch on.

Isn't Japan Terribly Expensive?

This is the next question people ask after I tell them how much money they can make. That's why I always put my answer in terms of how much you can *save* as a teacher in Japan. The answer depends on the area you live in, the amount of time you put into your work and your ability to save. I was able to live quite comfortably and still save at least $1,000 a month. My monthly budget was as follows:

Monthly Budget		
Rent	¥45,000	($409)
Utilities	10,000	(90)
Food	45,000	(409)
Misc.	20,000	(181)
Total	¥120,000	($1,090)

I didn't live in Tokyo so my rent of ¥45,000 ($409) provided a nice two-room apartment in a good location. In Tokyo you can get housing for about the same price but you probably won't get your own two-room apartment. The utilities included gas, electric, water and phone (I quickly learned to curtail my international phone calls!). My food budget might have been a little on the high side because I almost always ate out (I'm not much of a cook) and this account included my bar tab. Miscellaneous included all the incidentals and entertainment that one needs to survive. I lived comfortably, ate well, had a great time and still saved well over $1,000 a month.

On the other hand, a co-worker who lived in the same neighborhood didn't save a cent. He enjoyed spending his money. He is still in Japan, and still loves it. The size of your savings account will depend on your ability to save.

What Is It Like to Live in Japan?

The answer to this question will always be subjective. Some people describe Japan in only favorable terms, while others seem to dwell on the most bizarre aspects of its culture. Therefore, my advice is to gather as much information from as many sources as possible. This is my perspective on life in Japan:

SAFE. Compared to other countries Japan has a very low violent crime rate (although white-collar crime is the national pastime). In the wee hours of the morning, after a night of carousing, I could walk thirty minutes through town to my apartment without worrying about my safety. There aren't many American cities where I would feel comfortable doing that.

Unfortunately, as Japan becomes more internationalized, the streets are becoming a little less safe. It pays to be cautious, particularly for women. I know some women who have been hassled but fortunately it was nothing too serious. I recommend that women be cautious and use the same common sense as they would at home.

EASY TO LIVE IN. People who have lived in different countries say Japan is one of the easiest in which to live. It is a modern, industrialized nation. Despite the difficult language, the people are very helpful, and most Japanese speak at least a little English. Japan has also become very westernized, so any comfort you expect at home is available. The inexpensive, incredibly efficient and extensive public transportation system also makes life easier.

AN ADVENTURE. Living in any foreign country is an adventure and Japan is no different. Each day brings new challenges to face, information to learn and experiences to be gained. The difference between this adventure and those in other countries is that living in Japan is easier and safer.

THE PEOPLE. The people you meet, both the Japanese and other *gaijin* (guy-jean: foreigners), are a wonderful part of the Japan experience. The Japanese are friendly and hospitable. They often go out of their way to assist you and have a sincere desire to get to know you. I was practically adopted by a couple of families. Their warmth and hospitality were a comfort to this *gaijin* eight thousand miles from home.

Among themselves, *gaijin* create a unique little community. Because there are relatively few *gaijin* (especially outside of Tokyo), you get to know one another and depend on each other. I consider the friends I made to be the most valuable aspect of my Japan experience.

SOUNDS PERFECT. Life in Japan is not perfect. There are negative aspects, and you should have no difficulty finding writers and others who are willing to describe some of them. For example, the Japanese sometimes stare and point at *gaijin* as if we were animals in a zoo. It isn't so bad in Tokyo where *gaijin* are more common, but in other parts of Japan, where there are fewer *gaijin*, it is quite noticeable. At first this was kind of an ego booster, but after six months it became annoying.

Another annoyance for me was lack of space. Japan's cities are densely populated and have the lowest park acreage per capita of any industrialized nation. Japan can be a frustrating place if you occasionally need a lonely mountain top to contemplate life, but with a little effort and exploration you'll find some beautiful private places. I was able to find space and solitude with impressive scenery in the mountains and along the coast, only a short train ride from my apartment.

You may find some aspects of the Japanese culture downright disagreeable. But with patience, flexibility and a sense of humor, you can take the bad with a grain of "rice" and enjoy the many positive aspects of your Japan adventure.

How Do I Get a Job Teaching in Japan?

Reading this book is a great start. This is a brief outline of the process of getting an English teaching job in Japan. The details are in the rest of the book:

1. Prepare. Pay attention to the chapters "Qualifications and Experience" and "Preparing to Go."

2. Assuming you won't have a job when you arrive in Japan, you'll begin your survival phase. You'll be living in one of the world's most expensive cities until you find a job. Don't let this scare you.

3. Begin your job search in Japan by contacting the many schools that recently advertised job openings and other schools from the various lists you have compiled.

4. Schools invite you in for an interview. Some schools may ask you to come in on the same day you call, and most will invite you sometime that week.

5. You interview and impress the schools. They'll offer you a job: sometimes on the spot, always within a few days.

6. After you receive an offer, thoroughly evaluate the school and choose the best one for you. You'll be asked to sign a one- to two-year contract.

7. The school processes the paperwork necessary for you to obtain your work visa. (Technically you aren't allowed to begin work until you obtain your visa. Most schools, however, put you to work right away.)

8. In a few weeks, the paperwork for your visa will be ready and you'll have to leave Japan to obtain it. Most people go to Korea because it is an inexpensive trip. The Embassy usually issues your visa within a few days.

9. After you obtain your work visa you'll return to Japan and start (or resume) teaching . . . and make lots of yen!

2

Schools, Students and Teachers

The English Conversation Industry in Japan

English conversation is a big industry in Japan. Over 8,000 English conversation schools are cashing in on the Japanese desire to learn English. The *Wall Street Journal* described studying English conversation as "one of Japan's trendiest preoccupations, offering the allures of business success and fairy tale romance." While the students study English to achieve business success, the conversation schools are profiting. In 1991 these schools made over $24 billion.

The Schools

I make a distinction between what I call "language" schools and "traditional" schools. The language schools are the ones profiting from Japan's preoccupation with studying English. The traditional schools, by my definition, are the universities, junior colleges, junior high and senior high schools that provide traditional education for Japanese students.

TRADITIONAL SCHOOLS. The traditional schools hire thousands of English conversation teachers every year. The biggest single employer is the Japanese government's JET program, which hires over 3,000 foreigners annually to teach in the public junior and senior high schools throughout the country (see page 61 for more information about the JET program).

Private junior and senior high schools hire their own English conversation teachers, as do the junior colleges and universities. The JET program does not require previous teaching experience. The private schools, junior colleges and universities generally recruit teachers with an M.A. or previous experience in Teaching English as a Second Language (TESL). But as one former university English conversation teacher in Japan told me, what the universities recruit and what they get sometimes differs, implying that teaching positions at these institutions can be filled by teachers with fewer qualifications.

LANGUAGE SCHOOLS. The majority of the available teaching positions are found at English language conversation schools (from now on, I will call them language schools). Almost all language schools are commercial (for profit). Language schools come in basically two types: "company" (or "in-company") and "in-house" schools. The company schools specialize in teaching company employees at their workplace, with the client company picking up the tab. The company teacher goes to various companies to teach on-site. It's not uncommon for the company teacher to travel to three, four or five different companies each week.

At the in-house schools, the students come to the school to study and usually pay for the lessons themselves. The in-house schools vary in style; some offer gimmicks to fit the interest of every type of student. A few schools combine popular activities such as cooking or singing with English instruction. But most of the in-house schools avoid all the gimmicks and provide basic conversation instruction for students who want to communicate in English.

In addition to the company and in-house schools, conversation lounges, coffee shops and even bars offer the Japanese opportunities to practice English with a native speaker in a more informal atmosphere.

The Students

Don't believe anybody who tells you what a "typical" Japanese student of English conversation is like. The typical student doesn't exist. Ages, professions, abilities and motivations are very different, even within the same English conversation class.

While *sarariman* usually study English at the request of their companies, the in-house students' motivations for studying English conversation include professional need, desire to travel and prestige. Ages of in-house students range from 3 to 75 years and older. The parents of the 3-year-old want their child to have an advantage on the kindergarten entrance exams (which could determine the social status of their family for future generations), and the 75-year-old wants to keep his/her mind active.

Junior and senior high school students study English conversation for assistance on their university entrance exams, or to prepare for study abroad. College students study because they don't do anything else (their university years are the one time in their lives that the Japanese can relax), and English ability helps with job placement.

Office ladies (young women who work for a company and are relegated to the three *P*'s: phones, photocopying and pouring tea) study English because it looks good on their "marriage resumes" and helps when they travel abroad. Housewives study because it's fashionable and it kills an hour on Tuesday morning before aerobics class.

The Classrooms

The locations of these classes are as varied as the students. At traditional schools you teach on campus in traditional style classrooms. Company classes usually take place in a conference room on the premises of the client company. In-house school facilities vary from professional, spacious and comfortable classrooms to small, cramped, Spartan cubicles.

Part-time and private work will take you to more interesting locations. For private work, which means you are paid directly by a student, your apartment or the student's home is usually the classroom. Part-time work will usually be for an employer other than your sponsoring company, and you could end up teaching anywhere you can sit down. Coffee shops, bars or the back room of a beauty salon all make suitable part-time classrooms.

The Teachers

Your responsibilities as a teacher are fairly simple. The language school that hires you will provide all the training it deems necessary to make you a successful teacher (the universities, however, will expect you to step right in and begin teaching). At some small schools, training is limited to handing you a textbook and saying "*Gambatte!*"

(gam-baht-tay: work hard), but most language schools have an adequate training program.

WORKING HOURS. Language schools usually require you to be *available* for teaching assignments during certain hours of the day, such as from 9 a.m. to 9 p.m., and to *actually* teach a minimum of 20 to 40 hours a week. In addition to teaching, the school may require you to work office hours. During office hours you are supposed to prepare lesson plans or perform other tasks related to teaching. Other duties may include testing students and writing various reports. Traditional schools, on the other hand, usually have a set work schedule requiring you to work about 40 hours a week.

DRESS. Company teachers are generally required to dress professionally, i.e., a business suit is best. Men are asked to at least wear a tie and appropriate slacks. Women should wear equivalent business attire. Women in Japan usually don't wear slacks to work. The traditional and in-house schools usually allow teachers to wear more informal attire, but you still must take care to dress neatly and conservatively.

SATISFY THE CUSTOMER. The conversation school's priority may not be to improve the students' conversation skills. Consequently, your number-one responsibility is to keep the student as a paying customer. You will find your students' happiness is more important than their progress. English conversation in Japan is a very social affair. In-house schools often provide monthly or quarterly social events for their students, and your company students will frequently come up with reasons to have an eating/drinking party (with an emphasis on the drinking).

The students will have a keen interest in you. Japanese students traditionally have great respect for their *sensei.*

They also have an almost fanatical curiosity about foreigners, and you might even enjoy celebrity status.

The advanced classes usually consist of conversation. In these classes your role will be more of a facilitator than a teacher. You will work harder for your money at the lower levels. Japanese students aren't used to actively participating in learning. Getting them to respond can sometimes be a bit frustrating. Your school and fellow teachers will teach you how to coax your students out of their shyness. Patience, flexibility and a sense of humor will take you a long way as a *sensei*.

3

Qualifications and Experience

What You Need to Get Hired

The basic qualification for getting a job teaching English conversation in Japan is your native English-speaking ability. However, as with any position you apply for, the more applicable experience you have the better your chances of getting the perfect job and a higher salary.

Another requirement for most English conversation teaching positions in Japan is a degree from a university. The degree can be in any subject. A degree is necessary because Japan Immigration wants to see proof of it (your diploma) before it issues you a work visa. Immigration considers a degree (in any subject) to be the experience that makes you a qualified English conversation teacher and worthy of being allowed to work in Japan.

As I mentioned previously, and will discuss in more detail later, you can work legally without a university degree if you obtain a cultural visa.

The Current Job Market

Five years ago you could have landed a great teaching position in Japan with only native English-speaking ability and a university degree. Unfortunately the market has changed. The competition for jobs has increased.

With the advent of the U.S. and world recessions, more and more native English speakers who could not find work at home traveled to Japan to seek their fortunes in the English conversation industry. Then the Japanese "bubble" economy began to deflate, and companies and consumers found themselves with less cash to spend.

The result has been more job-seekers chasing fewer jobs. Wages have also leveled off a bit. But as you can see from the survey of the *Japan Times* help wanted ads and the example compensation packages in the Appendix, plenty of well-paying teaching positions are still available. The bottom line is that there are still lots of jobs available, but job seekers today need to be better prepared than their predecessors.

If you feel the only relevant experience you can put on your resume is your university education (and even that's in a non-related field), don't despair; you're probably overlooking teaching skills you have already acquired. And you still have time to gain applicable experience before you leave.

Applicable experience can also mean a higher salary. Any professional English language school should pay you more on the basis of your years of applicable experience. Bring documentation, such as a letter of reference or certificate, to verify your experience.

Before discussing the qualifications that will help you get a teaching position in Japan, here are a few more details on the two minimum requirements.

Minimum Requirements

NATIVE ENGLISH-SPEAKING ABILITY. You don't need to be a citizen of an English-speaking country; you only need native English-speaking ability. I know a few Germans with near native English-speaking *ability* who are teaching English in Japan.

Having native English-speaking ability doesn't mean you speak the way prospective employers would like you to. Strong regional accents are discouraged, but slight accents are acceptable. I know two *sensei,* one from Texas and the other from Boston, whose slight accents aren't noticeable to Japanese, and they had no problem finding jobs (however, they couldn't figure out how I got a job with my California accent). During interviews use professional language. Avoid using slang. Whatever lingo is trendy right now isn't welcome in the English conversation classroom in Japan.

UNIVERSITY DEGREE. Most English language schools in Japan could care less about the university degree. They're more interested in your personality, appearance and experience. Japan Immigration, on the other hand, is very interested in your diploma and wants to see this piece of paper before it issues you a work visa.

Your degree can be in any field. English language teachers in Japan have majored in such fields as Dance, Sociology, Accounting, Tourism, Criminal Justice—you name it. Language schools consider degrees in or related to Education, English, Business and Engineering the most appealing (Business and Engineering are favored because many of the students are business people or engineers). If you majored in something other than these four fields, you can still make your education work to your advantage during the interview.

Helpful Qualifications

If you can list some of the following qualifications or experience on your resume, you will be in a better position to convince the schools that you are the best person for the job. Also, the more experience you have, the better your chances for a higher salary. With a little effort on your part, you can acquire some of this experience before you leave for Japan.

PREVIOUS EXPERIENCE TEACHING ENGLISH IN JAPAN OR ANOTHER FOREIGN COUNTRY. This is probably the best experience you can have. Since you are reading this, common sense indicates you probably can't legitimately put "taught in Japan" on your resume. But if you happen to get some part-time work as a teacher in Japan before you join a school full-time (technically illegal, but . . .), be sure to let the hiring schools know this. Experience teaching English as a foreign language in another country would also be very helpful.

MASTER OF ARTS AND/OR TEACHING CREDENTIAL. A Master of Arts (M.A.) degree in Education or English, especially with an emphasis in Teaching English as a Second Language (TESL), is a definite advantage. This opens up the possibility for the better paying, more prestigious university positions. Jobs such as Head Teacher and other curriculum-related work at the larger language schools are also available to those with higher degrees in TESL. A teaching credential of any kind is an advantage, but if you have gone to the trouble of getting the credential, go a few steps farther and take at least a few courses in TESL.

Be careful that your education or teaching expertise doesn't backfire on you. Language schools don't want "know-it-alls" to come in and mess up a profitable system.

TESL OR TEFL CERTIFICATE. Many universities in English-speaking countries offer a TESL certificate or a TESL minor. If you can't complete the whole program, even a few TESL courses will look good on your resume. Some universities and junior colleges also offer TESL course work through extension or short courses. For example, the University of California at Berkeley now offers a TESL course specifically for people who want to teach English in Japan. Ask your local university or community college about their TESL courses.

Other organizations also provide Teaching English as a Foreign Language (TEFL) training and certification. The University of Cambridge Local Examinations Syndicate provides training and testing for a Certificate in the Teaching of English as a Foreign language to Adults (CTEFLA) at various centers throughout the world. This is an internationally recognized TEFL certificate.

The United Kingdom has hundreds of these schools but there are only four schools in the United States that currently offer the Cambridge course. One is in New York, another is in Southern California and two are in San Francisco. The names, addresses and phone numbers are listed in the Appendix. I am told that in the coming years the number of organizations offering TEFL or TESL training in North America will increase significantly as the demand for TEFL teachers worldwide increases.

The course for the TEFL certificate requires over 100 hours of study and costs approximately $1,500. If you can afford such an investment, the training and/or certificate would certainly help you with your job search in Japan. These TEFL schools also advertise that they can assist with job placement in various countries.

MASTER'S DEGREE. As with any job you apply for, a Master's degree in any field gives you an edge over job-seekers with only a Bachelor's. Again, if the degree is in one of the four "appealing" areas of study, that's even better. If you have a Masters in Business Administration (MBA), you can try to find work preparing Japanese for the Graduate Management Admissions Test (GMAT). Some say it is a lucrative market.

TEACHING EXPERIENCE OF ANY KIND. Don't sell yourself short when it comes to your previous teaching experience. If you've ever had to impart knowledge or skills to another person, you've been a teacher. Tutors, teaching assistants, recreation leaders, people who have trained new employees, and coaches of youth sports all have teaching experience.

If you need to, be creative when you describe your teaching experience. If the only work experience on your resume is a summer job at a fast-food joint where you had to train a new employee, describe this as an example of your teaching experience.

Tutoring for a literacy project would be a great way to gain some practical experience before you go to Japan. It would also give you a chance to see if you like teaching. Tutoring for a community literacy program can be directly applicable to teaching English as a foreign language because many of the people who attend such classes have limited English ability. Your local library either has a program or can direct you to one.

One TESL professional suggests that you try to find refugee or immigrant resettlement programs that assist recent immigrants settling into their new communities. These organizations are always in need of volunteers to assist with ESL training. Check with local church and civic organizations.

Finally, check to see if your local university has a language exchange program. In these programs foreign students are paired with native English speakers. The foreign student gets to practice English and the native student practices the foreign language. Check with your university's ESL Department. Try to get paired with a Japanese student. This will not only help your Japanese but may provide a useful connection in Japan.

WORK EXPERIENCE. Work experience of any kind is an advantage. Again, language schools like people who have experience in education, business or engineering. If your experience does not involve those fields, you can still manipulate it to make your experience sound perfect for teaching English in Japan. For example, a geologist I know convinced a school that his experience would be useful at the many steel and cement companies in Japan.

English language schools, like employers everywhere, prefer to see some stability in your work history. It looks good if you stayed with one company for a significant period, even if it was only a part-time job through high school and/or college.

OVERSEAS TRAVEL EXPERIENCE. Any overseas travel experience you have had shows the school you know how to survive in a foreign country and are less likely to leave without notice due to homesickness. On your resume mention any traveling you have done and emphasize overseas travel experiences during your interviews.

JAPANESE LANGUAGE ABILITY. You do not need to speak a word of Japanese to get a job teaching in Japan, but some schools will hire teachers with Japanese ability. This is particularly true of schools that include young children as students.

If you can list some of the qualifications or experience mentioned above on your resume, it will be very helpful when you look for a job teaching English in Japan. Take whatever time you need to gain some of this experience. The more ammunition you have the better. Be sure to get proper verification of any qualifications or experience in the form of certificates or letters from the organizations you worked for.

4

Preparing to Go

Very Important

You've decided to venture off to Japan and make lots of yen teaching English conversation. As the Japanese would say, *Gambatte!* Now it's time to prepare for this adventure.

If you have a valid passport, you could hop on the next plane to Japan, and you would find work eventually. This is not recommended. The smart approach is to allow yourself enough time to make preparations that will help you with your job search and life in Japan. Take as much time as possible to prepare for this adventure. The more time you spend preparing, the better your chances for a successful experience.

This chapter has two lists. The first contains tasks you *must* complete before you leave for Japan. The second is a list of preparations that will be very helpful in making your experience a success.

Tasks You Must Complete

PASSPORT. You must have a valid passport to enter Japan. United States citizens do not need, nor can they obtain, a tourist visa. When you arrive in Japan, Immigration will stamp your passport with a 90-day "Temporary Visitor Status."

For U.S. Citizens if you have never had a passport, call your local Post Office to find out where you can obtain and submit an application. Along with the completed application, you must also submit: proof of citizenship (birth certificate), proof of identity (driver's license or ID card), two passport photos and $65. Your passport should be ready within four weeks.

If you have a passport, check to make sure it will remain valid. If your passport has expired or you need to renew it, check with the Post Office for details.

> **Action**: Get your passport in order right away. This will be a symbolic act, demonstrating your resolve to go.

DECIDE WHEN TO LEAVE. When you leave home isn't as important as when you arrive in Japan. Some Japan experts say the best months for job hunting are January, April, July and September. An informal survey of the *Japan Times* help wanted ads from October 1991 through January 1993 shows that the demand for teachers seems highest from January through June. The help wanted ads temporarily drop off in May due to holidays and pick up again in June. Demand starts to taper off in July and hits a low in December. Complete survey results are in the Appendix.

If possible, try to avoid arriving on or near a national holiday. When the Japanese take a holiday, all 125 million of them take it at once.

January 1	New Year's Day
January 15	Coming-of-Age-Day
February 11	National Foundation Day
March 21 (varies)	Vernal Equinox Day
April 29	Greenery Day
May 3	Constitution Day
May 4	Citizen's Day
May 5	Children's Day
September 15	Respect-for-the-Aged Day
September 24 (varies)	Autumnal Equinox Day
October 10	Health & Sports Day
November 3	Culture Day
November 23	Labor Day
December 23	Emperor's Birthday

Japan's National Holidays

In addition to the above national holidays, there are three major holiday periods you definitely want to avoid because most English language schools are closed and it is impossible to find a place to stay:

December 20 to January 7, New Year's Holiday: The actual holiday period extends from the last few days of December to the end of the first week of January, but nearly all language schools shut down for a longer period. Almost no interviewing takes place during this period. The help wanted ads for teaching positions pick up immediately in the second week of January.

Last week of April to first week of May, Golden Week: A cluster of holidays is spread over these two weeks so it's easier for companies to shut down for a week or so. Many language schools also close. The problem for the job-seeking *gaijin* is that the whole country is traveling and it's tough to find a place to stay.

Mid-August, O-Bon: A Buddhist-based belief says all dead ancestors return during this period. The living pay respect by returning to their home towns. Avoid the second and third weeks in August.

Action: Try to avoid the holiday periods. When deciding when to arrive in Japan note the results of the *Japan Times* survey and realize that those months the "experts" recommend as the best for job-hunting attract the most job seekers. Pick a departure date that allows you adequate time to prepare.

AIRLINE TICKETS. Shop around, shop around and then shop around some more. Get the travel section from the Sunday newspaper and the *Yellow Pages*. Call every ticket agent who advertises discount tickets to Japan. Look for agents who specialize in travel to Asia. Don't rely on only one agent.

Discount tickets are usually round trip and have some restrictions. You have the advantage of being flexible about your departure date (within a few weeks). Tell the agent this and that you want the cheapest flight.

Buying discount tickets is tricky because of your return ticket. You'll be working for at least one year and will probably want to come home for the December holidays. If you don't have a job before you leave, you won't know your return date. The tricky part is that discount tickets usually require a specific return date within a limited period. A one-year open return ticket would be best, but this is a bit more expensive.

Work with the ticket agents. Let them know what you are trying to do, and have them find the most economical solution. You may find that it's more economical to buy a discount round-trip ticket even if you don't use the return ticket at all. Some people try to sell their return ticket after they arrive in Japan. Ask your agent if this is a possibility.

When dealing with ticket agents unfamiliar to you, the Better Business Bureau recommends:

- Verify your reservation with the airline before you pay the agent.
- Pay with a credit card. If a problem occurs, it's easier to cancel a transaction.

Action: Start shopping for your ticket right away, even if you don't have a departure date. Familiarize yourself with the market. Use the *Yellow Pages* and newspapers in large metropolitan areas for the largest selection of agents (also check with travel agents in Los Angeles and San Francisco because most Japan-bound flights originate from those airports).

UNIVERSITY DIPLOMA. Don't leave home without your diploma. This is your ticket to a work visa. Bring the actual diploma, not a photocopy. Japan Immigration knows a photocopy can be faked.

Get your other important paperwork in order. This should include a professional looking resume, letters of reference, certificates and other documents that prove your applicable experience. You need to bring only a few copies of each with you because you can easily have more copies made in Japan. One former job-seeker in Japan who lost one of his bags before an interview recommends that you pack a duplicate set of all important documents in each of your bags.

Action: Take your university diploma, a few copies of your resume and other documents. Put duplicate sets in different bags, including your carry-on.

CLOTHES. It's difficult to decide what clothes to take. You'll go through several different phases in a short time. During phase one of your Japan adventure you will be a budget traveler. Lugging numerous bags around Tokyo isn't fun. The train stations have coin lockers, but only a few are large enough to accommodate luggage and these are almost always full. If other storage services exist they are difficult to find. Many veteran English teachers have horrible memories of being burdened with too much luggage during their first few weeks.

Phase two is more complicated. You'll be a job-seeker as well as a low-budget traveler. In spite of living out of your bags in temporary accommodations, you will need pressed professional clothes for your daily interviews.

Phase three finds you as the newly employed English conversation *sensei*. You will be dressing professionally at least five days a week. The luggage you cursed every time you picked it up during your first few weeks in Japan now doesn't carry enough clothes to get you through a week of work.

Japan's four distinct seasons compound your packing dilemma. They range from a brutally cold winter in some parts to a summer that's oppressively hot and humid. And no matter what the season, it seems you can always count on some rain. Check to see what the weather will be like when you arrive in Japan and for the following three months.

Bring only what you need to survive and get a job. Dress clothes should be mix-and-match so you can have several fashion options and still remain economical with your luggage. Keep everything else to a minimum.

Pack the rest of your clothes (a year's worth) separately. The minute you have an address in Japan where you can receive packages, have your additional clothes sent to you. The U.S. Postal Service sends packages by surface mail. This takes from one to three months. A box that weighs 44 pounds costs about $95. The Post Office can send that same box airmail with delivery in about two weeks at a cost of around $275. Check with other delivery services to see if they can do it faster or more cheaply.

• *Very important*. When you arrive in Japan be sure to declare at Customs that you expect to receive "unaccompanied luggage." If the box arrives in Japan without this declaration on file, the "Honorable" Customs Agents will hold your package for a significant length of time while they ponder your letter of apology. For more information refer to the brochure "Customs Hints" from the Japan National Tourist Organization (see page 47 for information about this organization).

Take a three month supply of prescription medicines. By then you will have health insurance. Most prescriptions are available in Japan, except birth control pills. Take some pain relievers and vitamins; Japanese brands seem to be different from those we are used to.

Action: Pack lightly. You'll be traveling without a place to store your bags. Pack enough business clothes for a five-day work week. Pack your reinforcements before you go. Do some research. When you know your arrival date, see what the weather should be like. Ask the Post Office and other delivery services for their price and delivery estimates. Remember to declare your unaccompanied luggage at Customs in Japan.

Optional (But Highly Recommended) Tasks

If you do everything outlined above and none of the tasks listed below, you will eventually find work in Japan. Your chances for success, however, increase proportionately to the time you spend on the following tasks. It's a rule of life: the better prepared you are, the better your chances for success.

READ. Read everything about Japan you can get your hands on. To save money, check your local library first. Book stores have a variety of books about Japan, but be choosy about your selections. A few books recommended by veterans of the Japan experience include:

> *The Japanese Mind,* by Robert C. Christopher. Published by Fawcett Columbine. I consider this a must-read. As the jacket cover claims, this book "Illuminates every aspect of Japanese life and culture."

Max Danger and *More Max Danger*, by Robert J. Collins. Published by Charles E. Tuttle Inc. These two books by this former columnist of the *Japan Times* present a very humorous, but accurate look at life in Japan through the eyes of a *gaijin*.

Learning to Bow, by Bruce Feiler. Published by Ticknor & Fields. A well written account of a JET teacher's stay in Japan. Provides an interesting and humorous look at the Japanese culture, its school system and students' psyche.

You Gotta Have Wa, by Robert Whiting. Published by Vintage Books. A must-read for baseball fans. Even if you aren't a fan, you should still read this book for its insightful observations of Japanese culture.

Polite Fictions: Why Japanese and Americans Seem Rude to Each Other, by Nancy Sadamoto and Reiko Naotsuka. Published by Kinseido in Tokyo. The authors explore cultural differences between Japanese and Americans.

Japan, a Travel Survival Kit, by Robert Strauss et al. A Lonely Planet Publication. This budget travel guide explains everything you need to know about surviving in Japan. No matter which travel guide you buy, I recommend that you read this before you leave.

When buying travel guides stick to those that market themselves as *budget* travel guides. Check the year of the latest printing. The guide book should be current within a year or so. Information changes rapidly and an outdated book won't be helpful.

A few books deal specifically with teaching English in Japan. John Wharton's *Jobs in Japan*, published by Global Books, was considered by many to be the "bible" for prospective English teachers (until this book came along). Some of the information is outdated and a little too rosy for the current market, but you should read it before you go to Japan. These are some other books about teaching English in Japan:

Teaching English in Japan, by Jerry O'Sullivan. Published by Brighton. Provides an in-depth look at life in Japan, including a lot of details on culture and customs. The best half of the book is devoted to the actual teaching of English in Japan.

The Job Hunter's Guide to Japan, by Terra Brockman. Published by Kodansha of Japan. Explores job possibilities in various fields. Has one chapter that provides a slightly different perspective on teaching in Japan, so it's worth reading.

Teaching English Abroad, by Susan Griffith. Published by Petersen Guides. Explores English teaching possibilities throughout the world. It has a very good chapter on Japan.

A Guide to Teaching English in Japan, compiled and edited by Charles Wordell and Greta Gorsuch. Published by the Japan Times. This is not a job hunter's guide, but a collection of essays discussing issues relating to English teaching in Japan. The essays present a different and sometimes not very positive perspective on teaching English in Japan. It does have some good information about useful techniques for teaching English conversation.

If you can't find these books at the library or your local book store, check with Kinokuniya or Asahiya Book Stores (locations are listed in Appendix). These stores stock thousands of books about Japan.

Try to read all of the books listed above (most can be found at various libraries) and more. While at the library spend time browsing through periodicals for articles dealing with various aspects of Japan. The more you read the less "culture shock" you'll experience when you arrive in Japan. Don't worry, no matter how much you read, there will still be plenty of culture shock to keep life interesting.

Although I can't recommend any specific books on the subject, check out some books that deal with teaching English to foreigners. Your local library will have several.

Action: Begin reading about Japan when the thought of teaching English in Japan first enters your mind. Read your budget travel guide in its entirety before you leave.

WRITE. There are many organizations you should write to, or if you can afford it, call. The Appendix lists the addresses and telephone numbers of organizations you should contact. These organizations can help you with everything from reserving accommodations to providing job leads.

The first organization to contact is the Japan National Tourist Office (JNTO), which promotes and facilitates travel for foreigners in Japan. They provide valuable information that will help you survive in Japan until you are employed. JNTO offices are located throughout North

America. If possible, visit a JNTO office. Ask JNTO for the following brochures and information:

- "Economic Travel in Japan": tips for the budget traveler in Japan
- "Japan Travel-Phone": details about the English phone help line and other useful information
- Tourist maps of Tokyo and Japan, in English
- A list of inexpensive places to stay in Tokyo and other cities you know you will visit
- A youth hostel map of Japan
- "Hospitable and Economical Japanese Inn Group": a guide to Japanese *ryokan* (Japanese-style bed and breakfast inns)
- Japan Railpass information
- "Customs Hints for Visitors": a brochure providing customs information for entering the country
- A railway timetable in English

Finally, ask for any additional information for the budget traveler.

In addition to JNTO, try to contact all the organizations mentioned throughout this book. The phone numbers and addresses for all of the organizations are listed in the Appendix. Information is a powerful tool—gather as much as you can.

Action: Contact the organizations right away; some organizations take time to respond. If you can afford it, a phone call is usually more efficient.

NETWORK. Japan is held together by its networking system, and to be successful you must develop your own. Your network should begin at home. Start spreading the word that you are heading for Japan. You'll meet many people who have either been to Japan or know somebody who has. Nearly every day I meet somebody who knows somebody who has taught, or wants to teach English in Japan. My doctor's cousin, the person who drives my sister's friend to the airport and two of the many salesmen I encountered recently while buying a car all knew somebody who has been to Japan. When you hear of somebody who has been to Japan, ask if you can talk with them.

Ask these veterans of the Japan experience all of your silly questions. Ask if they think the advice in this and other books is good. Veterans of the Japan experience love to talk about their adventure, but they don't get enough opportunities. They may even provide you with some job leads.

You should also try to meet Japanese in your country. If you can make friends with some Japanese, this could be a real bonus when you venture to their country. Start with organizations like the Japan Society that are located in large metropolitan areas. Look in the white pages of your telephone book for the Japan Society and other Japan-oriented organizations. College campuses usually have international centers or Asian clubs. Make an effort to get involved—it will pay off.

Action: Tell everyone you know and meet that you are going to Japan to teach English. Whenever somebody says his/her second cousin (or some such connection) has done this, ask to speak with this person. Make an effort to meet Japanese.

JAPAN RAILPASS. Japan Railpass is similar to Europe's Eurail pass. It allows you to travel on almost all of Japan's railways at no additional cost. The cost of a 7-day pass is ¥27,000 ($245), a 14-day pass is ¥44,200 ($402) and a 21-day pass is ¥56,600 ($514). The actual dollar amount of the pass will vary depending on the current exchange rate. If you plan to do any traveling, the rail pass is a must. You should also consider purchasing a pass if you know you don't want to work in Tokyo but aren't sure where in Japan you want to live.

Note: you can only purchase the pass *outside* of Japan, so you must purchase it *before* you leave home. JNTO can tell you where to purchase the pass.

> **Action**: Get information regarding rail passes from JNTO. See page 76 for strategies on how to get the most value from your rail pass.

YOUTH HOSTEL CARD. Youth hostels are some of the most inexpensive places to stay in Japan. Hostels in Japan aren't strict about the card, but you can save a few yen if you have one. Check with a local International Youth Hostel for details on obtaining a card. In the U.S. you can contact American Youth Hostels, Inc.

> **Action:** Write to American Youth Hostels, Inc. for a youth hostel card. Ask JNTO or write directly to Japan Youth Hostels for a Japan Youth Hostels map (address in Appendix).

RESERVATIONS. Make reservations for your first three nights in Japan. It's a terrible feeling to fly for 12 hours and then find out at 8 p.m. that there's no place to stay under $150. Do this at least two months in advance. You'll find a suggestion for your first couple of nights in Japan on page 76.

> **Action:** Using the information from JNTO and your guide book, decide where you want to stay and make reservations. The information from JNTO provides details on how to do this by mail.

INTERNATIONAL DRIVER'S LICENSE. You may never get a chance to drive in Japan (or want to), but you might want to be prepared if the opportunity does arise. Some schools in outlying areas offer the use of a car as part of its compensation. Having an international driver's license allows you to drive without going through the complicated process of obtaining a Japanese driver's license.

> **Action:** Call your local department of motor vehicles or automobile association for information.

THE LANGUAGE. Learn as much Japanese as you can. You don't need to speak one word of Japanese to teach or live comfortably in Japan (Have you read this enough times?); but the more Japanese you know, the easier it will be to survive, live and prosper in Japan.

Knowing just a couple of Japanese words can turn a very frustrating experience into an only slightly frustrating experience. At the beginning of my Japan adventure, riding the train was always exciting because I was never a hundred percent sure I was on the right one. After learning the Japanese word *ma-de* (ma-day: to), I never again arrived at a "mystery" location. With this single Japanese word and the name of my destination, my success rate of getting on the right train skyrocketed. If I was going to the Ginza station, I would simply ask anyone in the vicinity, "Ginza *ma-de*?" (To Ginza?), and he/she would point to the correct train.

Some books recommend that at the very least you learn *kata-kana*, one of two Japanese syllabaries. *Kata-kana* is used to spell foreign words that are not originally part of the Japanese language. For example, the word "hamburger" becomes:

ハンバーガー

ha n bah gah

You are supposed to learn this alphabet so you can order food in places like McDonald's.

If you are going to spend only a little time studying Japanese before you go, I think it's better to concentrate on learning survival phrases rather than *kata-kana*. Every restaurant in Japan (including McDonald's) has either a picture menu or a life-sized plastic replica of every dish on the menu; so, if you have the ability to point, you can order without reading *kata-kana*. You'll eventually have to learn *kata-kana*, but if your time is limited, I suggest that you concentrate on survival phrases. The Appendix has some survival phrases that you can start with.

Action: At the very least, learn some Japanese survival phrases. Although you don't need to speak Japanese, the more you know, the better off you will be.

FINANCES. Get your finances in order before you leave home. Ask a trusted family member or friend to act as your financial guardian. Keep a checking account open and give your guardian signing authority.

Take a major credit card with you. Credit cards aren't widely accepted in Japan (especially at the budget places), but if you need additional money it will be important. Maintain the billing address in your home country; a billing address in Japan may make the credit card company nervous. Have your credit card and other bills sent to your guardian. Make sure your checking account has enough to cover any monthly minimum payments. Later, when you start making lots of yen, you will pay those debts off in full.

Action: The above is just a suggestion. You need to give some thought to your finances so you can devise your own system. Too many people don't think about financial arrangements until the last minute and then they panic. You will owe your financial guardian a big bottle of sake and dinner at an expensive Japanese restaurant upon your return.

MONEY. The old saying "It takes money to make money" applies to teaching English in Japan. Some Japan experts estimate it takes from a minimum of $1,500 to as much as $5,000 to get to Japan and survive until you receive your first paycheck. The minimum figure is probably too low, especially if you include the cost of the flight. The maximum figure might not be unreasonable if you include the costs of settling in. Still, with $5,000 you would be surviving quite comfortably (see the sample survival budget on page 90).

You can count on needing between $2,000 and $4,000 for this investment. And it is an investment. You can expect to recoup more than a reasonable return.

Action: Using the information in Chapter 6, "Surviving in Japan," and your other resources, determine your financial needs and save accordingly.

O-MIYAGE (OH-ME-YA-GAY: SOUVENIR). This is the Japanese equivalent of a souvenir. Bring some *o-miyage* with you to Japan. You will meet many Japanese who will go out of their way to help you. It's a very nice gesture to give them a little present, and it goes a long way in developing your network. *O-miyage* also come in handy when you are settling in and meeting your neighbors.

You will be packing light so you don't need extra weight. Small *o-miyage* like pens, pins or key chains from a famous city near your home are perfect. One enterprising (and cheap) prospective *sensei* called her local tourist office before she left, and they provided her with many little trinkets emblazoned with the city's name on it for free. She was very popular. You can also check with your local Chamber of Commerce.

Action: Bring some small, inexpensive *o-miyage.*

That's it. There really isn't that much to do before you leave for Japan. Do take the time to prepare. It will save you time, money and frustration after you arrive. The amount you save should be directly proportional to the amount of time you spend preparing for this adventure.

5

Where to Find the Jobs

From Home and in Japan

Now to the "meat and potatoes," or if the Japanese had an equivalent saying, the "sushi and rice" of getting an English conversation teaching position in Japan. You can secure teaching jobs both within Japan and from your own country. However, the majority of the available positions are filled in Japan.

The competition for securing a position outside of Japan is incredible. Thousands of people would love to teach in Japan if they could secure the job from home. One major language school that recruits annually in North America recently received over 4,000 applications for 20 positions.

In spite of the competition, you should still make an effort outside of Japan. Even if you are unsuccessful with this initial job search, you'll get a better understanding of the English conversation industry and its hiring process.

You'll also develop connections for your network; every school that recruits outside of Japan also hires in Japan.

There are some trade-offs to signing a contract with a school outside of Japan. Before I suggest organizations to contact and places to look for job leads, I'll discuss some of the trade-offs that you should consider before committing to a school from outside of Japan.

Trade-offs of Getting the Job from Home

PRE-EMPLOYMENT SURVIVAL. By getting hired at home you avoid many of the hassles (challenges) everyone who goes to Japan to look for work must face. The school that hires you outside of Japan should help you with everything from obtaining your work visa before you leave to providing a place to stay for your first few nights in Japan.

You won't, however, get to experience the challenge of surviving until you find a job, an experience many veteran English *sensei* consider the most memorable part of their adventure. Some *sensei* actually consider the challenge of surviving and prospering in a completely foreign environment the primary purpose of their adventure.

INITIAL INVESTMENT. Securing the job from home should greatly reduce your investment. When you arrive without a job, you must survive until you start receiving a paycheck, and Japan isn't a cheap country in which to survive. It's also common for a school that hires you outside of Japan to pay your air fare. By getting your job before you leave, you could save several thousand dollars.

The down side is that you can expect less compensation than if you signed a contract in Japan. Salaries are usually lower for *sensei* who are hired outside of Japan. Some say that this is a fair trade-off, if you consider the lower initial investment. Check the contract, especially the compensation package, carefully before you sign it outside of Japan. Compare it with the sample packages included in this book, and then decide if the lower salary offsets your reduced initial investment.

YOUR WORK VISA. Securing your position from outside of Japan eliminates all of your visa hassles. You'll enter Japan with your work visa in hand. *Sensei* who get the job in Japan must leave Japan to obtain their work visas. This means a quick trip to a country like Korea. If you sign an employment contract outside of Japan, obtaining your visa before you enter Japan is a pro with no con.

THE UNKNOWN. When you sign a contract outside of Japan you don't know what you're getting yourself into. You won't know much about the school, your co-workers or the area where you'll be living. Most people wouldn't buy a car sight unseen, yet many commit a year or more of their lives to a situation they know nothing about.

Some schools recruit outside of Japan so they can place teachers in less than ideal situations. They're trying either to pay a smaller salary or to place the teacher in an area that, for some reason, isn't popular with foreigners.

Be wary of the recruiter. Sometimes the person doing the hiring outside of Japan is a professional recruiter and is not an employee of the school. The recruiter makes money by delivering a body to Japan. This person may not have your or the school's best interests in mind.

Consider these trade-offs before signing a contract outside of Japan. Try to talk with someone who was hired outside of Japan and get her/his perspective. This may be difficult since few people get their teaching jobs outside of Japan. If you are lucky enough to get an offer while still at home, be very inquisitive before making a commitment to that school.

Starting the Job Search from Home

As I mentioned earlier, the competition for getting a job teaching English from outside of Japan is difficult. Thousands of people are applying for relatively few positions (compared with the number of positions filled in Japan). You should still make the effort before you leave for Japan. You may get lucky and land a job; at the very least you will learn a lot more about the industry and its interviewing process.

COMMERCIAL LANGUAGE SCHOOLS. Commercial language schools that recruit outside of Japan range from the very large to the very small. Two well-known language schools, AEON and Sony Language Laboratories, recruit in North America annually. Write to them and other schools listed under "Job Hunting from North America" in the Appendix. You will probably get a response.

You could also try to reach other schools by writing to them in Japan. Unless they specifically request letters, this is a long shot. You could send letters to schools with addresses listed under "English Conversation Schools in Japan" in the Appendix asking about their current hiring situation. A standard letter to Japan costs fifty cents. Don't be disappointed if the response is limited from this list.

• *College campuses.* Some language schools recruit on college campuses. Stay in touch with your local campus career placement center and TESL Department. Ask your career counselor if they have information about teaching in Japan. Most university career centers have information on teaching abroad. Also keep an eye on the college newspaper's help wanted ads.

• *Help wanted ads.* Sony, AEON and other schools advertise in the large metropolitan newspapers. The ads usually appear in the help wanted ads, under the headings of "Teacher," and you should also check the headings "English," "Instructor" and "Education."

Japan! Japan!

AEON, one of the largest English conversation schools in Japan, currently seeks enthusiastic professionals to teach English in one of our 180 branch schools located throughout Japan. Recruitments are conducted on a regular basis. BA/BS degree required. ESL teaching experience preferred. These positions are salaried and offer benefits and housing assistance. For consideration, please send resume and one page essay stating why you want to live and work in Japan To: AEON INTERCULTURAL CORPORATION, 9301 Wilshire Blvd., Suite 202, Beverly Hills, CA 90210 (EOE).

Teachers/English

SONY Language Lab seeks classroom teachers to work in Japan. 20 hours per week, and overtime available. Applicants must hold a Bachelor or higher degree from accredited college/university. ESL/EFL experience helpful. (Please do not call until after the March 20th deadline). Pending April 1994 hire on yearly contract. Send resume and cover letter to: MS. T. ARISAKA, SONY CORPORATION OF AMERICA, 9 WEST 57TH ST, NEW YORK, NY 10019 by March 20, 1993. An Affirmative Action/Equal Opportunity Employer M/F/D/V.

SONY

TEACHER, ENGLISH - wanted in Japan. FAX# 011-81-734-25-6420 or Write: KGG Foreign Lang. Institute, 1 Nishi-Takamatsu, Wakayama City

TEACHER of English in Japan. Pref exp w/nursery, pre-K, or K-12. Music a definite plus. 1 yr contract. Start 6-1-93. BA, US passport, age 23+. 250,000 yen/mo, visa, housing, bnfts, bonus. Private school, 20 yrs in Western Tokyo, starting new kiddie classes. Resume: Personnel Dir, MIKE'S ENGLISH SCHOOL, 150 Powell St #403, SF 94102

Help Wanted Ads from North American Newspapers

UNIVERSITIES AND PRIVATE SCHOOLS. English language teaching positions at universities and private schools usually require a Master of Arts in TESL or a related field of study (remember what my friend said about what the universities say they want and what they will accept). Most of the hiring is done in Japan, and most of the schools begin recruiting in January and February for the start of the school year in April, although some start recruiting as early as October. Note that the school year in Japan *begins* in April. These institutions sometimes advertise in large metropolitan newspapers in North America but it is more common for them to recruit on college campuses, especially those with a reputation for a strong TESL Department.

• *Teachers of English to Speakers of Other Languages, Inc.* TESOL is the number-one source in North America for teaching position leads at Japan's universities. TESOL has the stated mission "to strengthen the effective teaching and learning of English around the world . . . TESOL promotes scholarship, disseminates information, and strengthens instruction and research." TESOL publishes the *Placement Bulletin*, a bimonthly listing of English teaching positions available throughout the world, most of which require an M.A. in TESL. A year's subscription is $12. Write and ask for more information.

• *Japan Association of Language Teachers.* JALT, based in Japan, is a cousin of TESOL. JALT publishes a newsletter listing available teaching positions specifically in Japan. Write to them for more information.

• *The Times Educational Supplement.* This is a weekly published in London by Times Newspapers. It carries ads for teaching positions throughout the world, including Japan. Check your university's library to see if they have it.

JAPANESE EXCHANGE AND TEACHING PROGRAM (JET). In 1987, the Japanese government created the JET program to promote English language learning and international exchange with Japan. In 1993, JET recruited 2,087 foreigners, 1,075 of whom were U.S. citizens. They joined 1,698 teachers in Japan who were already working under the JET program.

Most JET participants work as Assistant Language Teachers (ALTs) in junior and senior high schools. To be an ALT you don't need to be a trained ESL teacher. The only requirements for ALTs are that you be a native speaker of standard English, a citizen of one of the six eligible countries (United States, Canada, Australia, New Zealand, United Kingdom, and Ireland), have a university degree and be under the age of 35.

The program teams the ALT with a Japanese English teacher. Working conditions can be pleasant or challenging. The attitudes of the assigned teacher and the school are important, but you won't know about these until you arrive. I have heard both positive and negative feedback from previous JET teachers, but nearly all agree that it is a good way to get your feet wet in Japan the first year and then move on to other work.

The JET program takes care of its ALTs. The program assists its teachers with transportation costs, processing visas and obtaining housing. They take a lot of the anxiety out of the Japan adventure, and the salary is competitive. The after-tax annual salary for ALTs in 1993 was about ¥3,600,000 ($32,727). This comes to ¥300,000 ($2,727) a month on the basis of a 40-hour work week. You are expected to pay your own rent and health insurance.

Applications for the JET program are available in late September or early October from the Japanese Embassy or Consulate. The deadline for submitting applications is the middle of December. Interviewing takes place in February. Successful candidates are notified in March. New recruits leave for Japan the middle of July. The contract is for one year and can be renewed. For more information write or call the Japanese Embassy or Consulate in your area. See the Appendix for addresses.

YMCA. The YMCA is a non-profit organization that runs English schools throughout Japan. While most of the hiring is done in Japan, it recruits about 55 teachers annually from North America for teaching positions in both Japan and Taiwan. The YMCA's International Office for Asia, located in Seattle, handles the recruiting.

The YMCA of Japan offers an extremely competitive compensation package that includes a salary based on applicable experience, assistance in finding a furnished apartment, payment of key money (apartment deposit) and round-trip air fare. The application deadline for YMCA positions in Japan is early October for placement in April . When you write to the Seattle office, ask for the "J-1" application.

YOUR NETWORK. Another source for job leads outside of Japan is your network. You should be searching out and meeting many people who have taught English in Japan. Ask them to write to their former employers on your behalf for current hiring information (you'll pay the 50 cents postage!). A letter from a former employee who left in good standing will definitely get a response. If your Japan connections do not feel comfortable writing to their former schools, at least get the phone number of the school and the name of a contact person from them so you can call when you arrive in Japan.

Do not underestimate the power of a good network. You should really make an effort to develop connections.

All networking requires is meeting people, and any good teacher should have no problem meeting people. You can do it!

One friend recommends plugging into the computer networks to find out what's currently happening in Japan. I am not that familiar with the new computer networks, but my friend has provided me with current news from job hunters and teachers in Japan by accessing CompuServe. I have even seen a few teaching positions posted. If you have access to a computer and one of these electronic mail networks, use it.

THE JAPAN TIMES. The number-one source for teaching position leads in Japan is the Monday edition of the *Japan Times.* This is an English daily published in Japan. You can find the *Japan Times* at any major train station in Tokyo, but it's a little more difficult to find outside of Japan. Check with your local and university libraries to see if they have it. Also contact the Japanese Embassy or Consulate; they usually have a library that carries the paper.

When checking with libraries or consulates, make sure to specify the *Japan Times* daily. The Japan Times also publishes a weekly magazine style paper that's widely available in libraries, but the weekly doesn't have the help wanted ads.

You can order specific copies of the *Japan Times* from two companies in California. In San Francisco contact OCS America and in Southern California you can order a copy of the daily from the *Japan Times Weekly* office in Costa Mesa (they have a toll-free number). The cost is about $5 for one issue. Telephone numbers for both companies are listed in the Appendix. Be sure to specify the Monday edition!

The Monday edition of the *Japan Times* has want ads for positions currently available in Japan. This may not do you much good while you are still at home. You probably wouldn't be immediately available for an interview or to start the job, as most schools would require. Still, it's a good idea to take a look at a copy or two to see what the current employment market is like. You should also make a list of the schools that advertise and call them when you get to Japan. If the school gives an address in the advertisement, write to them.

ENTHUSIASTIC Native English Teacher for Children, Adults, Companies. Full-time; sponsorship, furnished apartment, competitive salary, paid vacations. Shizuoka. PLS (0544) 26-0555.

NATIVE English Teacher for children to adults. Full/Part-time. Driver's license required. Sponsorship available. "R" Foreign Language Institute. Phone/Fax 0485-81-1975. Tobu-Tojo Line, Yorii, Saitama.

FEMALE English Conversation Instructor wanted. Full-time employment. Okayama Prefecture. Call Joëlle Kokumai: (0868) 23-2284. Passe-muraille Language School.

FULL time English teachers needed in Urawa (20 min. from Ikebukuro). Sponsorship available. Call Ms. Nasu 11:00 a.m.-9:00 p.m. IN English School 048-829-2360.

NATIVE ENGLISH TEACHERS needed in Tokushima. Fax resume to 0886-55-4868 or call 0888-46-0414, 20:30-23:00 ALFIE LANGUAGE.

FULL-TIME ENGLISH TEACHER wanted to start now. We are looking for a motivated and energetic native English speaker with a college degree and a good sense of humor. Age under 30 preferred. Competitive salary, paid training and paid vacations. Position offers an apartment and visa sponsorship. Experience not required. Please call Ms. Kudoh between 1 and 6 p.m. at 0471-67-5443 Promesa.

PART-TIME ENGLISH TEACHER wanted in Edogawa-ku. Please call on 03-3804-2565. Mon.-Fri. 5:00 p.m.-9:30 p.m. Oxbridge English School.

More Ads Following Page

Help Wanted Ads from the *Japan Times*

NATIVE English Instructors. Part-time ¥3,000/hr. Full-time min. ¥250,000/month. Extensive training, convenient locations. Competitive remuneration and sponsorship provided. Must have university degree. Positions in Osaka, Kyoto, Nagoya. In Osaka, call Ms. Nojima 06-372-0805, 10:00-17:00. BI-LINGUAL LANGUAGE INSTITUTE.

ENGLISH TEACHER wanted in southern Fukushima. Furnished apt., tel., and car provided. (0249) 52-6822. R & B English School.

URGENT: English Teacher wanted in Sendai. Call 022-252-3233 (Mon. to Sat./2:00 p.m.-8:00 p.m.). Saintpaulia English School.

TEACHING IN ATTRACTIVE HOKKAIDO Reliable school needs native English teachers. Call EC Inc. (011) 221-0279 for Tokyo Interview.

BRITANNICA — Recruiting a highly motivated native English instructor for our Nagoya Adult school. Experience and Degree necessary. Full-time position avail. Call Fiona Duncan at 052-951-4016 or fax resume to 052-951-7602. Office is closed on Mondays.

URGENTLY NEEDED! Japanese Language Teachers. Experienced or new. Training course available for those interested in entering this exciting field. Contact Mr. Kikuchi, Amica. 5484-0963.

NATIVE ENGLISH TEACHER wanted. Full/part-time. Age over 23, with degree and teaching experience. Accommodation provided. English House Utsunomiya (0286) 36-6579.

FULL-TIME native English instructor. Proper visa, tertiary qualifications, teaching experience. Salary ¥250,000~. Housing, holidays provided. Start mid. July. Send resume and photo to: Cosmo Language School, 4-20, Suehiro-cho, Kiryu-shi, Gunma-ken 〒376. Tel 0277-43-5700, Fax 0277-46-0795.

CHEERFUL English instructor required for family type school. Sponsorship available. Please send your resume and a photograph to A & S, 2-33-5-1007, Nozawa, Setagaya-ku, Tokyo 〒154.

ENGLISH SCHOOL BICS in Saginuma (30 mins from Shibuya/Denen-toshi line) needs native American/Canadian teachers (Full time or part time). Free use of sports club. Call Ms. Matsuoka, 044-854-3718 for interview.

The Job Search in Japan

NEWSPAPERS. You have just learned that the number-one source for open teaching position leads in Japan is the Monday edition of the *Japan Times*. You and every other job-seeking *gaijin* in Japan will pick up a copy first thing Monday morning and start calling in response to those advertisements.

Odds are you will get your job through one of these advertisements, but don't rely solely on the *Japan Times*. A few other English dailies carry advertisements, but none to the extent of the *Japan Times*. It won't hurt, however, to check the *Daily Yomiuri*, the *Mainichi Daily News* and the *Asahi Evening News,* all English dailies. The availability of these newspapers is not as good as the *Japan Times*, but if you ask around you will find them.

Check out the classifieds before purchasing the paper. Newspaper vendors in Japan don't usually care if you quickly peruse the paper before deciding to buy it. When you are about to invest as much as a dollar and a half (more for the *Japan Times*) you want to make sure there are at least some help wanted ads in the newspaper.

COLD CALLING. Your next source for jobs is the lists of schools found in this and other books. Also, while you were still at home, you developed your own list of schools from the *Japan Times*' help wanted ads you read and the schools mentioned by the veteran *sensei* you talked to. Call every school on every one of your lists. Local calls in Japan are only about eight cents (even cheaper with a phone card, see page 74).

I call this cold calling because you don't know if the school is in need of teachers at this time. When you make these calls you'll often hear, "Not hiring—click." You may get lucky, though, and call an office that just 30 minutes earlier decided to hire a new teacher. In another 10 minutes they were going to call the *Japan Times* to place a help wanted ad. You saved them the cost of an ad and the bother of all those interviews! This scenario isn't too strange. Luck and timing are important elements for any success.

If you do hear "Not hiring," don't throw away the phone number. Keep the phone number of every school that recently advertised and every school on every one of your lists. Call all of them every week or so. Hiring needs can develop at any time. Schools that recently recruited might find themselves in need of another teacher a few weeks later.

Many of the schools you will call are national, multi-branch schools. Like every bureaucracy, the left hand doesn't always know what the right hand is doing. Even if the head office in Tokyo says they aren't hiring, try the local offices in the various cities.

NETWORKING. Networking is probably the number-two source for job leads in Japan. It may even rival the *Japan Times.* Take advantage of anybody who offers to help you. Be pleasantly aggressive about networking. An effective networker doesn't wait for the network to develop around him/her.

When a school tells you they don't have an opening, ask if they know anybody who is currently hiring. As with any industry, competitors occasionally pal around, and they definitely know what the competition is doing. *Gaijin* personnel are more forthcoming with such information than the Japanese.

Leads come from odd places. If you are staying at a *gaijin* house (a hotel/apartment for foreign travelers and workers—more about these on page 77), some of the occupants may be teachers. Get information from them. Half of the *gaijin* at the hostels will be looking for work so they may be more tight-lipped with their information. Find out where the *gaijin* hang out and meet people there. More than one successful job lead has originated over a cup of coffee or a beer in a bar. Be open to every possibility, and be persistent.

THE KIMI INFORMATION CENTER. The Kimi Information Center, located near the Ikebukuro Station in Tokyo, is a good resource for job-seeking *sensei*. The Kimi Center has accommodations (usually filled) and provides office help (they have word processors, fax, photocopying, a message center and can provide you a mailing address). The services are reasonably priced. They also publish a newsletter that lists several job possibilities. The phone number is listed in the Appendix under "Assistance via the Telephone."

INTERNATIONAL CENTERS. In cities outside of Tokyo check to see if they have an international center (the tourist information offices in the various cities can tell you). Nearly all of the major cities and many of the smaller ones have an international center (part of Japan's committment to Internationalization). The centers' primary goal is to facilitate their communities' understanding and interaction with foreign countries and their citizens. Besides being a wonderful resource for the traveling or new *gaijin* in town, the centers usually have a bulletin board or newsletter where the local language schools post help wanted ads.

6

Surviving in Japan

What to Do Until You Find a Job

If you aren't one of the few who get a job before you leave for Japan you will have to "survive" in Japan until you start receiving a paycheck. This means surviving in the land of the infamous $4 cup of coffee. Don't despair. Using the information in this chapter, your budget travel guide and help from JNTO you can get by on as little as $30 a day.

Surviving in Japan until you find work will be the toughest, most exciting and most memorable part of your Japan adventure. You will be going alone to a country over 8,000 miles away from home where the language resembles nothing you have heard before. In Tokyo you will be living in the world's most expensive city. You will be traveling among over 12 million people packed into the world's most efficient transportation system, a system whose map resembles the diagram of the arteries of the human brain.

Sound like a nightmare? It's not—it's a challenge. When you think about surviving in Japan until you find a job and it begins to seem like a nightmare, remember that thousands of others before you have succeeded at what you are attempting.

One of those successful teachers who worked four years in Japan provides this advice: "Just think of the whole thing as an adventure. Decide how much money and time you can commit to this adventure, prepare for it and then take off. If your time and/or money runs out, your adventure is over."

Webster's Dictionary defines "adventure" as "an unusual, stirring experience often of a romantic nature." This is all you are committing yourself to.

The key to surviving in Japan, both before and after you are employed, is to have the right attitude. Patience, flexibility and a que sera sera philosophy will get you a long way (a sense of humor also helps).

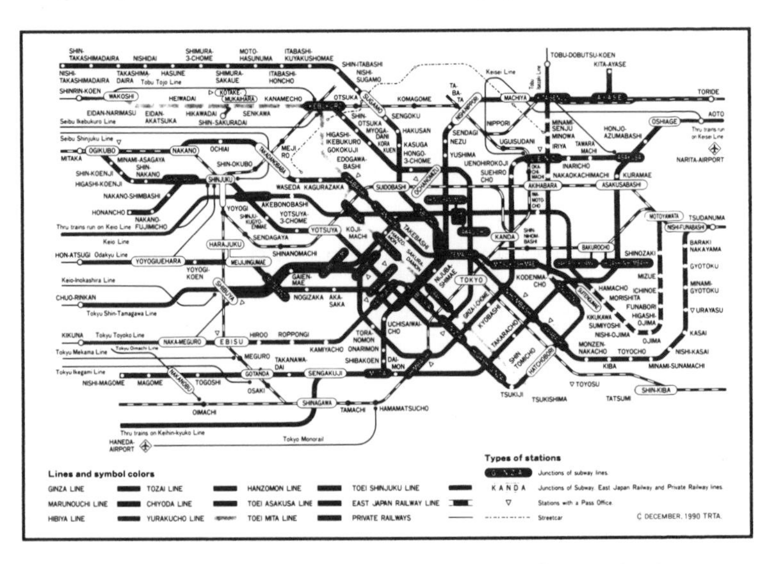

A map of the subway/train system – or the human brain?

This chapter provides some advice, hints and suggestions to help you make it through your first days in *Nihon* (knee-hone: Japan). Don't use this as your master plan. Develop your own plan, using information from this chapter, JNTO and your guide books. Whatever your plan is, keep it flexible.

On the Plane

The flight from the west coast of North America to Narita International Airport takes over 11 hours. Dress comfortably so you can rest, but neatly so you won't cause any second looks from the Japan Immigration or Customs officers. I have seen some scraggly looking *gaijin* subjected to very thorough searches at Customs. Avoid this by having a neat appearance.

Get as much sleep as possible on the plane. It takes a minimum of 18 hours and possibly up to 24 hours from the time you start your journey from home until you are finally in your room in Tokyo. Avoid too much alcohol on the plane. Your body doesn't rest well when it is fighting the effects of alcohol, even when you pass out. Do drink plenty of fluids (water & juice) because the extended period at high altitude tends to dehydrate you.

At Narita International Airport

Narita is a disappointment for the first-time visitor to Japan. In spite of being a world economic leader and a whiz at technological gadgetry, Japan has a surprisingly drab major international airport. In December 1992 the airport opened Terminal 2, with amenities that include easier access to the Narita Express train (see page 75), shower facilities and a place to nap. The best part is that it will ease the crowding in the original terminal.

IMMIGRATION AND CUSTOMS. Your first stop will be Immigration (if not the rest room after drinking so much liquid on the plane). It's quite a hike from the plane to Immigration and Customs; just follow the crowds.

Have your passport and customs declaration forms ready for the Immigration and Customs officials.

The Immigration officer may or may not ask you the following questions, but you should be ready with these answers:

Immigration: *Why are you in Japan?*

Answer: *Just traveling.*

(Don't mention anything about looking for work! Technically you are not allowed to enter Japan to look for work, and immigration will be the only one who cares that you are.)

Immigration: *How long are you staying in Japan?*

Answer: *About two months.*
(Remember, if you enter Japan with a "Visitor Status" you can only stay for 90 days)

Immigration: *Where are you staying?*

Answer: Have the address and phone number of your first night's lodging available.

The Immigration officer may ask you a few more questions. The whole exchange should last about thirty seconds. Be polite and patient. When he has finished with his questions, he'll stamp your passport with a 90-day "Visitor Status" visa exemption. You now have 90 days to become employed (and obtain your work visa) or exit the country.

Next, on to Customs. This should be no problem since you are traveling so light you will have nothing to declare. Many books recommend that you bring in your total duty-free allowance of three liters of alcohol and two cartons of cigarettes to use as gifts. I brought it all and ended up carrying all that extra weight for a month. I sold one of the bottles, drank the other two and smoked the cigarettes. You decide if the extra weight is worth it. Declare everything you do have. Also remember to declare unaccompanied luggage. Don't try to bring any funny stuff (drugs) in. The Japanese are very serious about this – ask Paul McCartney and Mick Jagger. Have a neat appearance, be patient and polite—you won't have any problem.

The Immigration and Customs officers will be the first Japanese officials you encounter. Always remember this extemely important rule when dealing with anyone who is in an "official capacity" in Japan: in any disagreement or misunderstanding, they are always right. It's cultural. They can't lose face. Even though a five-year-old would realize that you're right, arguing with Japanese officials will get you nowhere. Apologizing profusely is your only means to a favorable conclusion.

You cleared Immigration and Customs—Welcome to *Nihon*! Before you venture outside of the fortress they call Narita Airport (security is extremely tight), you should make a couple of brief stops.

CHANGING $ TO ¥. You may have already exchanged some greenbacks for yen before you left home, but you usually get a more favorable rate in Japan. If you need some yen stop by the currency exchange office at the airport. The rate won't be as good as at the large Tokyo banks, such as Sumitomo, but it should be better than rates at home.

THE TOURIST INFORMATION CENTER (TIC). Your next stop is the Tourist Information Center (TIC). This is a cousin of the JNTO and has three offices in Japan. One is located at Narita Airport, another is in downtown Tokyo and the third is in Kyoto. Much of the information will be the same as JNTO provided, but you will be able to pick up very valuable maps to specific places like the youth hostels, Kimi Information Center and other important destinations.

TELEPHONE CARD. At the TIC ask where in the airport you can buy a telephone card. Telephone cards are a wonderful convenience. Callers use these credit-card-size cards instead of coins in the pay phones. In addition to the convenience of not having to fish for coins, you also receive a discount on the cost of an already inexpensive call. A local three-minute call is only ¥10 (9 cents). With the card the cost per call is even less.

You can buy the cards at convenience stores and vending machines located near the pay phones. Buy the largest denomination available, which should be ¥3,000 ($27). This may seem like a lot of money for phone calls, but in the coming weeks you will spend all of it. By buying this denomination you receive ¥500 ($4.55) worth of free calls! The cards always have a picture of some beautiful or famous spot in Japan, so they make nice souvenirs to send to your family and friends when you have used them up.

VERIFY YOUR RESERVATIONS. After you buy the telephone card call the place you have reserved for your first night's lodging to make sure they still have a room for you. You have already made a reservation and confirmed it, but confusion may prevail. If your room isn't available, it's better to find this out while you are still at the airport where they have room reservation assistance.

From Narita to Your Room

GETTING TO TOKYO. Getting to Tokyo from the airport is no small undertaking. The Narita Express (NEX) train is the fastest, most convenient and most expensive way to get to Tokyo. It costs ¥2,890 ($26) and takes 76 minutes. The boarding station is located directly beneath the airport so no shuttle buses or transfers are involved. After 16 or more hours of travel the speed and convenience may be worth a few extra yen.

Depending on your budget and destination there are several alternative ways to get to Tokyo, including trains, buses and combinations thereof. Tickets range from ¥900 ($8) to ¥2,890 ($26).

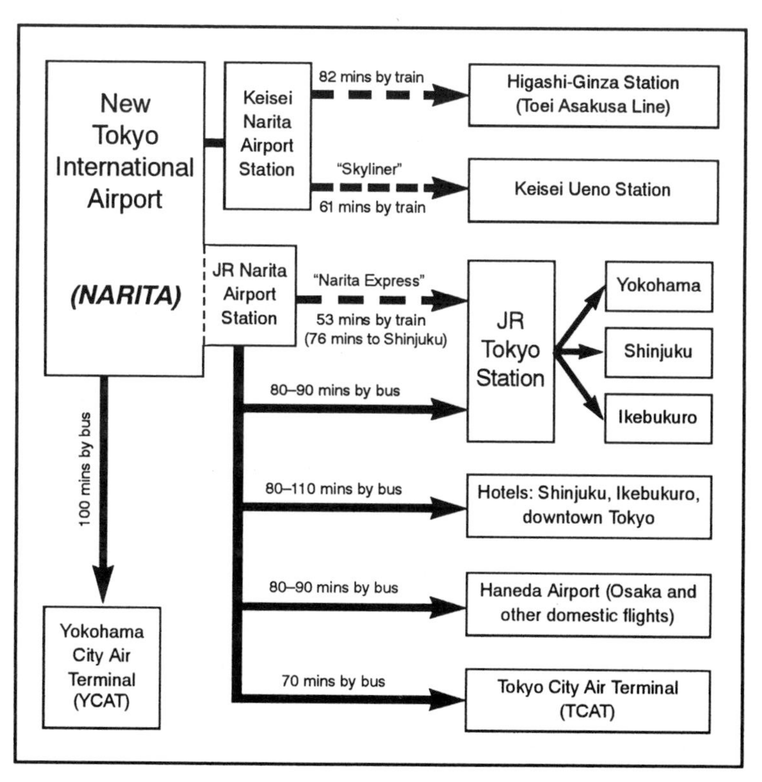

Transportation from Narita Airport

JAPAN RAILPASS. If you have a voucher for a rail pass, you have an important decision to make. You can turn your voucher in at the airport, receive your pass and ride the NEX to Tokyo for no charge. The problem is that the pass is good for only a limited number of continuous days. If you activate the pass at the airport you'll use up one day and only save the cost of NEX, about ¥3,000 ($27).

Real savings start when you take longer trips on the Shinkansen (bullet train). For example, a round trip to Osaka costs ¥27,000 ($245). After a week or so of job hunting in Tokyo, you can activate your pass to explore opportunities in other parts of Japan. On the other hand, if you know you will be traveling right away, activating the pass at the airport might not be a bad idea. Develop a rail pass strategy and make it worth your investment.

WHERE TO STAY. Your guidebook and JNTO list many inexpensive places to stay in Tokyo. For your first three nights you might want to consider staying at the Tokyo International Youth Hostel. This well-kept and comfortable facility is conveniently located within a few minutes walk of Iidabashi station in central Tokyo. Four people share a room, with separate facilities for men and women. The cost for one night, without meals, is ¥2,500 ($22).

Hostel purists believe this hostel is too nice and the staff too formal. They have strict rules: doors locked at 10:30 p.m., lights off at 11:00 p.m. and guests out by 10:00 a.m. There's a trade-off between the convenience and the rules. The first few nights in Tokyo you'll want something conveniently located and you'll need your rest.

You can only stay in this hostel for three consecutive nights. They are sometimes flexible about this rule, if they aren't full and you are extremely polite. You can reserve a room in advance by sending two international reply coupons (available at your local Post Office) to the hostel.

Yoyogi, on the west side of town, is the other youth hostel in Tokyo. It's actually the former dormitories of the 1964 Olympics. They haven't done much maintenance to them since 1964, so they're not as clean, nor do they have the amenities of the other hostel. The location isn't as convenient as the other hostel either, but it is slightly cheaper and beds are more readily available.

Your First Few Days in Tokyo

ACCOMMODATIONS. On your first morning in Tokyo your number-one priority is to secure future accommodations. Your guidebook and JNTO (or the TIC) should list plenty of inexpensive places. Call about availability and then visit the facility. The really inexpensive places may not be the kind of lodgings you want.

Your guidebook should give you a good description of various types of lodging and prices. Your choices vary from hostels, hotels and *ryokan* (ree-yo-cahn: Japanese-style bed-and-breakfast inns) to *gaijin* houses.

Gaijin houses offer shared communal-type accommodations. You can stay from one day to indefinitely. Daily rates are about ¥2,000 ($18) but few *gaijin* houses offer accommodations for just one night. Weekly and monthly stays are more common and those rates can be as low as ¥8,000 ($72) for a week and ¥35,000 ($318) for a month, usually for a shared room. Many *gaijin* like the few rules and communal atmosphere at these places. JNTO has a list of inexpensive places to stay that includes several *gaijin* houses.

Wherever you stay, make sure your accommodations for the near future are reserved at least three days in advance. During the weekends and holidays it can be impossible to find accommodations in Tokyo. If you leave

Tokyo make sure you have room reservations for your return. It's an empty feeling to arrive in Tokyo late in the afternoon with no place to stay and no vacancies.

Leaving Tokyo can also provide you with a place to sleep. If you travel to other parts of Japan check the overnight buses or ferries. The buses are first class, complete with fully reclining seats, a television, stereo and refreshments. They get you to your destination and save you the cost of a night's lodgings as well. Ask the TIC or a travel agent for more information.

ORIENT YOURSELF. Familiarize yourself with the Greater Tokyo Area. Go to tourist attractions to practice using the trains/subways and your navigation skills. Visit the major districts including Shinjuku, Ginza, Roppongi, Shibuya and Ikebukuro. You'll probably go to each of these districts for interviews.

Go to the TIC in Tokyo. You already received information from JNTO and the airport TIC, but you still need to see the Tokyo TIC. It's the largest TIC and provides room reservation assistance. Every time you are near the TIC pick up a map of Tokyo and a laminated pocket-sized map of the subway and train system; you will constantly wear these out (you saw a reduced black & white copy on page 70).

You should also visit the Kinokuniya Book Store in Shinjuku (a district in western Tokyo). This book store is affiliated with the Kinokuniya stores in the United States, and it carries the largest selection of English books in Tokyo.

Find out where you can buy the *Japan Times*. On Monday this will be important for your job search. Most major train/subway stations carry it, but make sure you know where you can get a copy.

Communicating

Japan is an easy country to live in without speaking the language. Many *gaijin* spend years in *Nihon* without learning a word of Japanese (truly a waste; don't let this happen to you). This is because so many Japanese can speak some *Eigo* (ay-go: English). Nevertheless, every day you'll find yourself in situations that require you to communicate your needs without the advantage of sharing a common language. With patience it's easy. This is important advice when you try to communicate with the natives: be patient.

WHOM TO APPROACH. When seeking information in *Eigo* most books recommend that you approach either older students or younger professionals. The reasoning is that they are most likely to be current with their English studies. Don't limit yourself to these groups. You will be surprised at the variety of Japanese who can, and want to, speak *Eigo*. A Japanese friend of mine, who is now teaching at a U.S. university, told me that when she was in Tokyo she hoped that *gaijin* would ask her for assistance so that she could use her *Eigo*.

SPEAK CLEARLY AND SLOWLY. Keep your sentences short and simple, like you are talking to a 3-year old. You may feel a little condescending, but you won't be offending the person you are trying to communicate with. No need to raise your voice; yelling doesn't facilitate understanding.

Speaking English with the Japanese is a skill you will develop over time. In the beginning you should make a conscious effort to communicate on the simplest terms.

"NO ENGLISH!" If the response to your initial inquiry of a Japanese person's English ability is in Japanese and the person holds her/his hands in the sign of an "X," this means the person doesn't or is afraid to speak *Eigo*. This doesn't mean you should end attempts to communicate. You can try some of the following:

• *Use one word.* Reduce your communication to one word. For example, the most important question in any language, "Where is the rest room?," can be conveyed by simply saying, "Toilet?" (Don't say bathroom. Americans are the only people who refer to the place you bathe as the same place you relieve yourself.)

• *Use hand gestures or pantomime.* Try to use hand gestures with one-word sentences. For example, if you need to find a razor in a store say "Razor?" and pantomime shaving.

• *Write.* An effective way to communicate is by writing the word or sentence in English. Remember, almost all Japanese have studied English for at least six years, entirely in written form. Although their ears may not understand what you are trying to say, their eyes may have an easier time.

• *Use a dictionary.* Before you leave for Japan be sure to buy an English/Japanese dictionary. Always keep it with you. Before you become a serious student of Japanese, look the word up in English, and then show the person with whom you are communicating the word in Japanese. Don't try to pronounce it yourself: this may cause more confusion and some giggles at your expense.

Some travel guides provide translations or detachable cards you can show to somebody. For example, "Where is the train station?" is written in Japanese, and you simply show this to somebody for assistance. The Appendix has Japanese translations for some useful survival phrases.

My final recommendation is to learn Japanese! As I told you before, it will make your life easier while in Japan. It also won't hurt in your life after Japan.

Directions

This may appear to be an odd heading but it really is important. As Dave Barry explains in his book, *Dave Barry Does Japan:*

> Something like 15 million people live there, and at any moment, 14.7 million of them are lost. This is because the Tokyo street system holds the world record for randomness. . . . This is one of the biggest, busiest, most important cities in the world, and most of the streets don't have names.
>
> But wait! There's more. On these streets without names there are buildings with meaningless numbers . . . So getting to an unfamiliar destination in Tokyo is basically a matter of going on the Treasure Hunt From Hell.

Mr. Barry makes a lot of money as a humorous writer, but he doesn't exaggerate too much. Addresses are useless in Japan. The easiest way to find a location is to have a map for your destination, get to the nearest subway station and start asking people the way. Tourist information pamphlets always include a map. If you don't have a map, get the following information when asking for directions:

- The name of the subway/train line you'll be taking.
- The name of the station where you'll be getting off.
- The number of the exit you will use to leave the station (sometimes there are dozens and exiting at the right one is critical).
- The nearest landmark. A business with an English sign is best. A Western fast-food place is a good landmark.

In addition to this information you will need explicit directions about how many blocks to walk, how many streets have signals, etc. Time estimates are also helpful. For example, "Walk three minutes down this street." Just hope your stride is the same length as the Japanese.

ASK A COP. Even with a map and explicit directions, odds are you will still get lost. Be patient. The best thing to do is find a police officer. With the low crime rate, the most important job of the police officer in Japan is to give directions. You can find the police in their little climate-controlled offices known as *koban* (co-bahn: police box). The *koban* are located at or near almost all subway/train stations, shopping areas and business districts. *Koban* are easily identified by the red light affixed above the door.

Show the police officer your map. If you don't have a map, neatly write down the name and address of your destination in English. Be careful trying to verbalize; your pronunciation of the location may be more confusing than helpful.

You can also try asking the average Japanese on the street. One problem with this strategy is that you may be given the wrong directions. The Japanese don't like to lose face by admitting they don't know where something is. It happens occasionally, but for the most part, the average Japanese is extremely helpful. Every *gaijin* has a story about a Japanese person who went 20 minutes out of her/his way to personally deliver the lost individual to the correct location.

When it's 3:20 in the afternoon and you're still looking for the office of your 3 o'clock interview, remember: patience, flexibility and a "Whatever-will-be, will-be" attitude are the keys to survival in the Land of the Rising Sun.

Transportation

Getting around Tokyo is really quite easy, although at times it can seem overwhelming. When it does, step back, take a deep breath and look at your map again. If this doesn't help, then ask somebody. Helpful Japanese are always nearby.

This discussion of the transportation system focuses on the subway and trains. The bus isn't recommended in Tokyo, and taxis are too expensive. Your travel guide should have more detailed explanations on the entire transportation system.

SUBWAYS AND TRAINS. Japan's rail transportation system is world renowned for its efficiency and punctuality. It's also user friendly, even for foreigners. Every major station in Tokyo has signs in *Eigo*. You may have to look carefully sometimes, but they are there.

The most important advice is to *stay off the trains during rush hour*. The most crowded hours are in the morning between 7:30 and 9:00. It isn't as bad in the afternoon, but it's best if you can avoid the hours from around 4:00 p.m., when the students are leaving school, until about 7:00 p.m., when the last of the non-drinking *sarariman* make their way home.

You must conquer three tasks to successfully ride the rail: buy your ticket, board the train and disembark at the right station. These really aren't difficult to master.

- *Buying your ticket.* First, you must buy your ticket. The fare board is above the ticket vending machines. This board is written in Japanese. Pull out your pocket-sized English map of the subway/train system and find your present location. Next locate the station you want to go to. Count the number of stops in between. Now look up at the board. A red arrow shows your location.

Count the number of stops to your destination. Notice the corresponding numbers; the smaller one is the child's fare and the larger one is your fare.

If determining the correct fare becomes too confusing, just buy the lowest-priced ticket. This allows you to get on the train. When you exit the system, the wicket man will ask you for the remaining fare. Don't be embarrassed; the Japanese do this all the time. You may also want to consider purchasing a subway pass. One-day or monthly passes are available. A one-day pass is ¥650 ($5.90) and a monthly pass is ¥15,800 ($143).

• *Boarding the train.* In the beginning, always check and double check before getting on a train bound for who knows where. The major stations will have signs in English that direct you to the correct platform, but in some smaller stations you might have to ask.

The first person to check with is the wicket person. This person punches your ticket as you enter the station. As you hand him your ticket just call out the name of your destination (if your pronunciation is good you can use the name of your destination, prefaced with the Japanese word *ma-de*). He will tell you in *Eigo*, or with a hand signal, the number of the right platform. It also helps to have a quizzical look on your face while you are asking. Many stations are now using machines instead of wicket men, but you should be able to find at least one station official who can assist you.

Once you are on the platform double check by asking either another station employee or a fellow passenger. Again, all you need to do is name your destination and point at the tracks you think the train will be arriving on. Hopefully you will be answered with an affirmitive nod of the head.

• *Disembarking.* Your next challenge is to get off at the right station. The platform signs have the station names in English, but sometimes these may be difficult to locate. On shorter trips you can just count the number of stops, but this can become tedious on longer trips. Use your pocket map to determine where you are. The newer trains have a map above the door upon which a blinking light indicates the station you are coming to.

You can also ask a fellow passenger. As you approach a station just point and say the name of your destination. Once you ask someone for help, he/she will usually make sure you get off at the right station.

This "rookie-on-the-rails" phase lasts only a couple of weeks at the most. In the beginning always allow yourself more than enough time to get to your destination. In other words, schedule in lost time.

Food

In Tokyo food can be your largest daily expense, even more than your lodging. If you're careful, you can survive on as little as ¥1,000 ($9) a day for food, but this is minimum subsistence. A reasonable daily food budget is ¥1,500 ($13.60). This is an example of a budget traveler's daily menu:

A Budget Traveler's Daily Menu

Breakfast: Banana and juice, ¥160 ($1.45).
Lunch: A set lunch at an inexpensive restaurant consisting of an entree, rice, soup, salad and pickled vegetables, ¥800 ($7.27).
Dinner: A bowl of udon (Japanese noodles), soba (buckwheat noodles) or ramen (Chinese noodles), served in a broth with other goodies, ¥500 ($4.50).

For an extra ¥500 ($4.50) a day you can eat really well, and even indulge in snacks and occasional Western-style fast food. With some effort you can get by on between 1,000 to 1,500 yen a day. However, you must know some tricks to accomplish this.

THE YOUTH HOSTEL. The Tokyo International Youth Hostel serves a hot meal with all the basics, including an entree, vegetable, fruit and all the soup and rice you can eat. Some dedicated budget travelers stock up on rice and soup at dinner and save the entree and some rice for the next day's lunch.

GROCERY STORES. An obvious place to find food is a grocery store. A not so obvious location for a grocery store is the basement of a glitzy department store, but this is where you find a *suupaa* (sue-pah: supermarket) in Japan.

Suupaa have all the food you would ever want. They carry the same fruit and vegetables you would find at home, but usually at much higher prices. For example, a honeydew melon costs about ¥5,000 ($45). Don't buy honeydew melons. On the other hand, pineapple and bananas are reasonably priced. Another good buy are *mikan* (me-con: An orange that resembles tangerines). The key to successful (i.e., inexpensive) shopping in the grocery stores is to try different foods and do a lot of comparison shopping.

A good way to try different foods, and also fill your stomach, is to take advantage of all the free samples. *Suupaa* offer samples of everything from meat to wine. You can make a meal of these samples at various grocery stores.

Besides the grocery, each department store usually has a floor dedicated to restaurants. See if they have any inexpensive eating places.

CONVENIENCE STORES. Convenience stores (including 7-11s) are everywhere. At these stores you can find almost all of the foods you would at an American store, but the bargains will be in the Japanese snacks. See the menu in the Appendix for the Japanese snacks to look for.

RESTAURANTS. Very important: unless someone else is buying, never eat at a restaurant that doesn't list the prices outside. Nearly all restaurants display life-size replicas of the dishes they serve in cases outside of the restaurant. If the prices are not listed with the replicas, don't go inside.

Be especially wary of the little "snack bars." These are drinking establishments that charge a sit-down fee ranging from ¥3,000 ($27) to ¥10,000 ($91) and more. And this doesn't include the cost of your drinks! Always ask "How much?" before you sit down at these places.

The restaurants you will frequent as a budget traveler won't look like much. They may only seat about 10 to 15 people and might not appear too clean, but they are cheap and serve good food.

• *Ordering.* Ordering at these places is easy. If you don't know the name of the dish, simply point to the plastic replica. One *gaijin* used to copy the name of the dish she wanted after looking at the replicas. This could be difficult if you aren't comfortable writing in Japanese, but it avoids taking the waitress outside to point at the replica.

• *Lunch specials.* Lunch is the best time to eat at a restaurant. This is when they have their specials. They usually sell a *setto* (set-oh: set lunch) or *teishoku* (tay-show-ku: another word for set lunch), which consists of an entree, rice, soup, pickled vegetables, and maybe a salad.

Look for a replica resembling a *setto*. If the price is right, go inside and say "Set-oh."

• *Morning service.* Also look for coffee shops that offer *moningu sabisu* (mo-ning-gu sah-bis: morning service). For the cost of an expensive cup of coffee you can also get an egg and toast for less than ¥500 ($4.50). Check the menu in the Appendix to see how "morning service" is written in Japanese and look for it in the coffee shops.

Other good places to get cheap, quick snacks are located at or near train stations. At various stands you can get a steaming hot bowl of udon, soba or ramen. You usually eat these standing up, elbow-to-elbow with harried *sarariman*.

The Appendix has a menu of other reasonably priced dishes written in both English and Japanese so you can just show the waitress what you want. Before leaving for Japan, it's a good idea to visit a few Japanese restaurants and familiarize yourself with the food.

VENDING MACHINES. These machines are everywhere and sell everything. The most common products sold are soft drinks, which cost ¥110 ($1). In other vending machines you can find everything from steak for tonight's dinner to flowers for a special occasion. Stick to buying sodas from the machines.

WESTERN-STYLE FAST FOOD. The number of Western-style fast-food restaurants in Japan may surprise you. You will see McDonald's and Kentucky Fried Chicken everywhere. You will also find Baskin Robbins, Mister Donut and some familiar pizza joints, among others. Except for the pizza, the food is identical to what these establishments serve in the West. The pizza ingredients are only slightly different (for example, they put corn and occasionally squid on otherwise perfectly good pizzas).

Prices at these places are higher than those at home. Still, your craving for something familiar will sometimes overcome your desire to save money. It's OK; just don't make a habit of it.

Pizza Hut and Shakey's can be economical places to eat. Both have all-you-can-eat lunchtime specials. This is a favorite of starving *gaijin*; ask your fellow *gaijin* where you can find one or the other.

You can also find economical fast foods by eating at places unfamiliar to you. Two popular Japanese fast-food hamburger places are Mos Burgers and Dom Dom's. Mos Burger has a sign that resembles the McDonald's sign and Dom Dom's has a red and white sign. Both are in English. The meat may take a little getting used to (apparently the cows are fed differently than North American cows; the meat's safe, it just tastes different), but both places are cheaper than McDonald's. There is also a Korean chain called Lotteria. Check the prices and compare. Remember, you get what you pay for.

JAPANESE-STYLE FAST FOOD. These restaurants serve a healthier and less expensive meal than their western-style counterparts. One of the most popular Japanese fast food chains is Hokka Hokka Ben. You can find them throughout Japan. These are take-out shops, usually consisting of only a counter, with no eating in. They have yellow and red signs.

The Hokka Hokka Ben Sign

Hokka Hokka has a picture menu on the counter and you just point to what looks good. They offer a *bento* (ben-toe: box lunch) which includes an entree such as sukiyaki, chicken nuggets, or fish with rice and a little salad. Curry rice and salads are also available. You can get a filling meal for ¥300 ($2.72) to ¥500 ($4.50).

When you eat in restaurants always drink water or tea. Don't waste money on sodas or alcohol. Another built-in money saver is that there's no tipping in Japan, anywhere. You don't tip in restaurants, bars, or taxis. Some of the newer western-style places like the Hard Rock Cafe encourage tipping, but when in Rome . . .

With a conscious effort you will be able to eat just fine on ¥1,500 ($13.60) a day while you are surviving. You will eat some different foods and in smaller quantities than you would at home, but your diet will usually be healthier, and nearly everybody can afford to lose a few kilograms.

Survival Budget

I've covered accommodations, food and transportation, which should be your major daily costs while surviving in Japan. The following is a sample daily survival budget that covers just those basics. I've estimated minimum and maximum daily expenditures.

Survival Budget

Food	¥1,500 ($13.60)	—	¥2,000 ($18)
Accommodations	2,000 (18.00)	—	3,500 (31)
Transportation	380 (3.45)	—	650 (6)
Total	¥3,880 ($34.00)	—	¥6,150 ($56)

Your transportation costs will obviously vary according to how much you travel each day. The minimum figure is the fare for one average round trip on the subway. The larger figure is the cost of a subway day pass. This budget doesn't include miscellaneous expenditures (telephone cards, post cards) or emergencies. Be sure to plan for those.

Assistance via the Phone

Several resources are available for your various needs. The Japanese understand that their language is very difficult for the traveling *gaijin* and have really tried to provide help for their foreign guests. All of the following organizations provide English-speaking operators whose only job is to assist foreigners in Japan. The phone numbers given below are for Tokyo; for phone numbers in other cities, please refer to the Appendix.

THE JAPAN TRAVEL PHONE: 03/3503-4400. Operators are available every day from 9:00 a.m. to 5:00 p.m. You should have received the Travel Phone brochure from JNTO. The brochure describes the service this way: "You might have some difficulty communicating with the local people or need more detailed information on the places or attractions you want to see. The Travel-Phone is your helping hand, ready to help you solve any problem or offer any travel information."

TOURIST INFORMATION CENTER: 03/3502-1461. You already know about the TIC (pages 74, 78). They can also provide information over the phone.

JAPAN RAILWAYS (JR): 03/3423-0111. This telephone service provides assistance with schedules and rail service information. It only covers the Greater Tokyo Area. JR does not operate the subways.

NTT INFORMATION: In Tokyo 03/5295-1010. Japan's national telephone company provides an *Eigo*-speaking operator, information on how to make domestic calls and assistance in obtaining phone service for *gaijin*.

Using the Phone

LOCAL CALLS. In Tokyo every phone number now begins with either number 3 or number 5 and all phone numbers have eight digits. If you are outside of Tokyo you must first dial area code 03 to reach Tokyo. In other cities area codes may be two to four digits, and most phone numbers outside of Tokyo will be seven digits. Note: if you call Tokyo from Narita Airport you must first dial 03 and then the number. If you have trouble completing a call within Japan call the NTT operator mentioned previously for assistance.

INTERNATIONAL PHONE CALLS. If you want to make an international call from a pay phone you must find one with a gold face. It will usually have a sign in English indicating it's an international pay phone. In Tokyo, international pay phones are everywhere but in the rest of the country they are a bit scarce. Most major subway/train stations have an international phone as do the major hotels.

- *Operator assisted.* For operator-assisted international calls by a Japanese operator dial 0051 and you will be connected to an English-speaking operator.

- *Home country direct.* If you want to make a credit card or call collect or person-to-person to your country you can contact an operator in that country by dialing the following numbers: For the U.S. dial 0039-111 to be connected to an ATT operator, and to reach Canada dial 0039-161.

• *Direct dial.* For international direct dial calls from Japan you can use your phone cards. Just as in the U.S., you must choose a long distance company. KDD is the best known long distance telephone company. Two other companies, IDC and ITJ, may be cheaper. The dialing codes for these long distance companies are:

KDD	001
IDC	0061
ITJ	0041

For direct dial international calls, first dial the number of your long distance company, then the country code ("1" for the U.S.) and finally the area code and number you are calling. For example:

0061 + 1 + (XXX) + 555-5555

0061 is the code for the long distance company IDC. 1 is the U.S. country code. The rest is the U.S. phone number.

Japanese Culture and Customs

Like every country, Japan has some unique customs. You will read about them in various books. In fact, whole books are dedicated to the subject of how to behave in Japan. You should probably read up on some of the Japanese customs, but don't become "customs paranoid," meaning you're afraid to do something for fear of offending somebody. The Japanese don't expect you to know or understand all of their customs.

Truth is, being a *gaijin* will work to your advantage. Since you are not Japanese and are not expected to behave in the same manner as the Japanese, you will be given a little extra leeway in certain situations. For now, follow two simple rules and you shouldn't offend anybody.

First, act and behave in a manner that would not upset your mother and you probably won't offend the Japanese. Simple enough. This means do not behave in the "ugly foreigner" role. Be polite, quiet and patient, and things will go smoothly.

Second, if you aren't sure of what to do or how to act in a particular situation, observe first. Watch how the Japanese behave in the same situation. Aren't sure if your shoes come off before entering a certain building? Watch somebody else do it. If you are confused about eating something with your fingers or chopsticks, take a look at the person next to you.

Following these two simple rules will ensure that you don't create any international incidents.

7

The Interview

Convincing the Schools to Hire You

It's been quite an adventure. Making the decision to come to Japan was tough. You're glad you spent all that time preparing, and it has paid off. You're surprised that surviving in *Nihon* isn't the nightmare you feared. Now comes the most important part of your adventure: convincing the schools you are the best person to teach English conversation.

The First Phone Call

When you're in Japan looking for a job, the interview process begins with your first phone call to schools that are currently advertising openings. In this industry interviewing and hiring happen quickly. In a normal job search (other than the English conversation industry in Japan), you submit a resume, and after a week or so the company might invite you to come in for an interview. In Japan you can expect the invitation to come after the first five-minute phone call.

During this phone conversation, the school will try to determine if you meet the basic requirements, have related experience and the right personality. You'll make your first impression on the phone. Keep your voice confident, pleasant and energetic. The interviewer will probably ask the following questions over the phone:

Interviewer: *What country are you from?*

Some schools might look for specific nationalities. The accent of choice is usually North American.

Interviewer: *What is your visa status?*

Some schools won't be interested in you without a work visa. Don't let this bother you. Such schools are small time. You wouldn't want to work for them.

Interviewer: *Do you have a university degree?*

Tell them you have your diploma with you. State the school and your major.

Interviewer: *Do you have any teaching experience?*

Describe your experience. Be brief. If you were a fast-food worker who trained new employees, tell the interviewer you were responsible for training new employees. During the first conversation elaborate only when asked. Point out any graduate degrees, certificates and relevant training.

Some schools will end the conversation at this point and invite you to come for an interview. Others may spend up to 30 minutes getting into questions usually reserved for the in-person interview.

A long phone interview works to your advantage. The more information you get, the better equipped you are to evaluate the school. If you decide that you don't like the school, it saves you a trip to the office for an interview.

Scheduling Interviews

Schedule your interviews carefully. Subway fare is at least a couple of dollars, and including travel time the interview could be a three-hour affair. Wise scheduling will save you some yen and time.

Before committing to a time, find out the location of the school. If by some miracle, the school is close to where you are staying, get an early appointment. Schedule interviews at offices across town later in the day when the commute is finished and you'll have time to find the office.

Review the section "Directions" on page 81. Receiving the directions over the phone means you'll be working without a map (if this sounds like a trapeze artist working without a net, it's for a good reason). Make sure the directions are clear. Get an address and accurate spelling for the school. You'll be showing several people this information during your search for the school.

The Interview

ARRIVE EARLY. Punctuality is an important attribute of successful teachers (although students will frequently be tardy, you try it once and you'll hear about it). Allow sufficient lost time when venturing to new areas. It's better to be extremely early than a little late. Stress that you know the importance of being on time.

WHAT TO TAKE. Take your resume, your diploma and other documents proving your applicable experience. The school may want to see your passport. If you don't have a briefcase, just take a file folder. Avoid lugging your day pack along; you want to look professional.

APPEARANCE AND PERSONALITY. Appearance and personality are very important in the English conversation industry. For your interviews, dress professionally and conservatively. For men a suit is best. Slacks, dress shirt and tie should be the minimum attire. Long hair and earrings on men are becoming more prevalent in the classroom, but are still unacceptable for the interview. Women should dress as you would for an interview at a bank. Nose rings and multicolored hair wouldn't be wise.

Presenting the right personality is more complicated. Schools look for such traits as professionalism, friendliness, patience and self-confidence. This pretty much describes you, right? Now convince the interviewer.

- *Professional.* Always conduct yourself in a professional manner. Be as polite and formal as the situation requires. Your speech and answers should help establish your professional attitude.

- *Friendly.* Don't be so stiff that your natural friendliness doesn't shine through. For you to be a successful teacher (and the school to be profitable), your students must like you. Let the interviewer see your friendly side.

- *Energetic.* Teaching requires a lot of energy. It's similar to performing on stage. Show the interviewer your positive, bright and engaging personality.

- *Patient.* Patience is an important asset when dealing with the sometimes painfully shy and insecure Japanese students. Show you are a patient person (don't let delays or interruptions during the interview fluster you). Discuss situations that have required you to be patient. For example, if you have dealt with irate customers or when you had to impart some knowledge or skill to another person.

• *Self-confident.* Be confident without being cocky. A teacher is a leader. Show the interviewer you're capable of standing in front of and leading a group of students.

Don't try to stretch your personality to convey all of these traits, but mention them as qualities you think are important in a good teacher. Discuss them as attributes you have used in different situations.

EXPERIENCE. Convincing the interviewer that you have the right experience to teach should be easy. You'll be well rehearsed when you describe how your experience makes you the best person to teach English conversation.

• *Education.* Tell the interviewer how your education prepared you for this position. As discussed earlier, the four most useful degrees in the eyes of the interviewer are Education, English, Business and Engineering. If you have a related degree, emphasize the similarities.

If you have a completely non-related degree think of a way to make it sound appealing. For example, if your major was Dance, explain how you are comfortable being in front of a group and leading people. If your degree is in Anthropology, your knowledge of different cultures gives you the ability to blend western-style teaching skills with Japanese-style learning. Mention applicable course work you have done. With creative thinking and wording, you can make any field of study seem perfect for this job.

• *Work experience.* When discussing your experience remember that teaching is "imparting knowledge or a skill to another person." If you don't have any real teaching experience, speak creatively about situations in which you did have to impart knowledge. Talk about the times you were a leader and worked closely with others. Discuss the people skills you have developed.

UNDERSTAND THE INDUSTRY. Let the interviewer know you understand the English conversation industry. It is a big business (this is true of the commercial schools, not necessarily the traditional schools). As a teacher in this business you have two goals. The first is to improve the students' English conversation skills, and the second is to keep the students as paying customers (for most commercial schools improving the students' skills isn't as important as keeping them as paying customers, but don't say that out loud).

To accomplish your goals as a teacher you need to establish a rapport with your students. Japanese students behave differently from Americans. They are reserved and are not used to participating. By using the right mix of friendliness, energy and understanding you can overcome their shyness and make the learning experience an enjoyable one. The Japanese are stressed out by every other facet of their lives; learning English should be fun.

You remember all the confusion you had as a foreign language student and what your teacher did to make you feel comfortable in class. Share this with the interviewer.

Tell the interviewer about your friends (the people from your network) who have worked in Japan. They told you a lot about the experience, so you have a good understanding of what it takes to teach and live in Japan.

In addition to teaching English conversation you will be expected to introduce your students to Western culture and traditions. For example, teaching the students how to shake hands; or how teachers and students interact in your culture. Be prepared to talk about this.

MAKE THE COMMITMENT. Language schools are wary of teachers who suddenly disappear without any notice. Assure the interviewer you'll honor your commitment to teach for the specified period or longer.

Have a good reason for wanting to teach and live in Japan. Money is a good reason (one the commercial schools should appreciate), but this shouldn't be your only reason. Your reasons could include a desire to learn about Japanese culture, business or language. Other *sensei* have wanted to use their teaching experience or gain some experience. Whatever your reason, be passionate about it. Convey that it's important enough for you to stay and achieve your goals.

On the other hand, make sure the interviewer knows you will always put the school and its goals first. This is a business after all, and you are a professional. You are fully aware that the school will be paying your salary and sponsoring your stay in *Nihon*. You will accomplish your personal goals on your own time.

You shouldn't have too much trouble proving your commitment to honor your contract. Considering the investment of time and money you have already made to reach this point, the air fare, new clothes and cost of surviving in Tokyo, you'll stay in Japan until you recoup your investment and then some.

One prospective *sensei* looked the interviewer right in the eye and stated: "I know you are concerned about teachers who leave without notice, but when I make a commitment I live up to it. If I promise to be here for two years, I will be here at least two years. If I get homesick, I will deal with it." She was offered the job.

OTHER TOPICS. Talk about your previous travel experiences. This shows you have lived abroad before, are aware of the potential pitfalls and can deal with them.

Read up on the latest fads in Japan. Magazines and newspapers in the West always have such articles. Golf is one fad that won't go away. If you're a golfer, tell the interviewer. Talk about other interests you share with the Japanese. Sharing the same interests helps you relate to your students.

OFF-THE-WALL QUESTIONS. The interviewer may ask some off-the-wall questions. This is especially true when the interviewer is Japanese (at the larger schools you'll usually have a native English-speaker as your interviewer, but at the smaller schools you will encounter Japanese interviewers). Go with the flow. You're interacting under different cultural rules, but don't put up with any offensive questions. You don't want to work for such a school.

Questions about your age and marital status aren't off limits in Japan. Age isn't important in the industry. The ages of *sensei* range from the recent 22-year-old graduate to the 50-year-old veteran. Age is a standard curiosity question of *gaijin*, so don't be offended when they ask.

Marital status is trickier. If you are married, your spouse should be with you in Japan and already employed. A distant or unemployed spouse isn't appealing to the school. If they ask about your boyfriend or girlfriend, just say you don't have one right now (even though you would rather tell them it's none of their business).

If all goes well they may offer you the job at the end of the interview. Don't accept right away. You have some evaluating to do. The more professional schools will invite you back for a second interview, and a few may ask you to do a demonstration lesson.

8

The Demonstration Lesson

Preparation and Presentation

Some schools may ask you to give a demonstration lesson before offering you the job. This is especially true of the commercial schools that don't require previous teaching experience. Don't be nervous. If you have been honest about your teaching experience, the school knows what to expect from you. The school just wants to see if you have the personality and basic skills to be a good teacher.

The following is basic information on how to prepare a lesson plan and teach English conversation in Japan. If you have formal training and/or experience in teaching, especially teaching ESL, you probably don't even need to read this chapter, except perhaps to get a feel for teaching in Japan. If you don't have formal teaching experience I recommend that you don't rely solely on this chapter for your training. As I mentioned in Chapter 3, "Qualifications and Experience," there are several ways to gain experience. You should at least go to the library and check out some of the many books that deal with teaching English to foreign students.

To give you an idea of what preparing a lesson plan and teaching a class are all about, I'll help you prepare a lesson plan and describe how you can teach it.

Before You Prepare a Lesson Plan

The school should give you at least a day to prepare your lesson plan. The "class" will usually consist of two to four members of the school's office staff. If they put you in front of paying customers, don't worry about it; the school is the one taking the chance. Before you prepare your lesson plan get the following information:

1. *How long will the lesson be?* It should be around 20 to 30 minutes, but find out what the school expects and make the class exactly that long.

2. *How many students?* You need to know so you can plan appropriate activities and prepare enough handouts (if you choose to prepare handouts).

3. *What is the students' ability level (beginning, intermediate or advanced)?* If the students have mixed abilities, which level should the lesson address?

4. *Will you be provided with a textbook or other specific material to teach?* If not, don't worry. This won't be a problem.

For this demo lesson let's assume that the lesson will be 20 minutes, that there will be four students (from the school's office staff) who are all at the beginning level and that the school is not providing you with a text or lesson objective.

Preparing the Lesson Plan

THE LESSON OBJECTIVE. The first thing you must do when preparing a lesson plan is choose a lesson objective. What are the students going to learn in this lesson? My number one rule for choosing a lesson objective (especially for a demonstration lesson) is: *Keep it simple.* Even if the school gives you a textbook and a specific chapter to teach, don't feel compelled to teach the entire chapter. Most English conversation books require about two hours of class time to teach one chapter. Choose a specific part of the chapter and concentrate on that.

In this example demonstration lesson you must choose the subject yourself. Keeping in mind that it should be simple and that your students are beginners, you have set your lesson objective as "Introductions." Actually, you could use this topic for any level of student and just increase the level of difficulty as necessary. This is a good subject for the demo lesson since you won't know the students and you will have to introduce yourselves.

THE LESSON STRUCTURE. Next, you will determine the lesson structure: How much time do you plan to devote to different segments of the lesson? I usually followed the following outline:

- Warm-up (15 percent of class time). The warm-up loosens the students up and gets them in the English conversation mode. This should be easy and fun.
- Main Lesson (35 percent). This is when you do your teaching and lay the groundwork to reach your lesson objective.
- Activity (35 percent). This gives the students an opportunity to execute what they have learned. This is usually an entertaining portion of the class.

- Closing (15 percent). This is the time to wind down and give you an opportunity to see if the students have achieved the lesson objective. Always have the students leave with smiles on their faces.

THE WARM-UP. Using the above as a guideline you can plan the lesson. The class is only 20 minutes so a warm-up would only be about 3 minutes. In this case you can simply introduce yourself and learn the students' names. It's important to use students' names to establish rapport, but since Japanese names seem to have about a hundred syllables, they are sometimes hard for the rookie *gaijin sensei* to remember. I usually asked the students to write their first names (that is, personal or given names, not family names—the Japanese consider their family name as their first name; good luck getting that straight) on a paper nameplate. You can make the nameplate by folding a piece of paper into thirds to create a triangle that will sit on the desk. Since this demo lesson is so short, you should prepare these before class begins and have them ready for the students.

THE MAIN LESSON. The main lesson will take about seven minutes. The goal is "Introductions" so you will use these key questions and phrases for the students to learn:

Q. What is your name?

A. My name is ____________________.

Q. Where are you from?

A. I am from ____________________.

Q. What do you do?

A. I am a ____________________.

You can introduce the key phrases ("My name is . . . ," "I am from . . . " and "I am a . . . ") by using them to introduce yourself and then writing them on the board. Have the students repeat the phrases as a group.

Next you can elicit from the students the appropriate questions for each of the key phrases and write these on the board. Eliciting (to draw out, or evoke) is an important teaching technique for foreign languages. You can use the prompting techniques discussed on page 110.

After the questions and key phrases are introduced you can verbally drill the students. Instead of asking each student yourself, you can try "chain drilling"; ask the first student the questions, then have that student ask the next until they have all asked and answered the questions. Monitor the students and correct them when appropriate.

Normally you would have the students work in pairs (pair work is important in the English conversation classroom), but this lesson is very short. If there is time you can have the students work in pairs to practice the key questions and phrases, and have them create one or two additional introductory questions on their own.

THE ACTIVITY. In this part of the lesson, have the students role-play. Ask two students to stand and introduce themselves using the key questions and answers. Each student will have an opportunity to ask and answer. Have the students role-play again, this time introducing themselves as famous people.

THE CLOSING. This will be about three minutes. Ask for questions, praise the students and thank them.

If you were to incorporate the above into a written lesson plan (which you should do, and give a copy to the person who is observing you) it would look like the following:

Lesson Objective: Introductions. Students will be able to ask and answer simple introductory questions.

Warm-up (3 minutes): Introduce myself. Students state their first names and write them on nameplates.

Main Lesson (7 minutes): Introductions

1. Teach the following key phrases:

   My name is ________________

   I 'm from __________________

   I am a ____________________

2. Elicit appropriate questions from students and write them on the board.

3. Drill the students. Ask one student the questions, then direct that student to ask the next student, and so on until all have asked and answered.

4. If there's time, have students do pair work to practice key questions and phrases and also create their own introductory questions.

Activity (7 minutes): Role Playing

1. Have students stand up, two at a time, and introduce themselves to each other, pretending that this is the first time they have met.

2. Have the students introduce themselves to each other as famous people.

Closing (3 minutes): Ask for questions, praise students and thank them profusely.

Example Demonstration Lesson Plan

Obviously, this is a very simple lesson that would probably be easy for any beginning student to grasp. That's OK for the demo lesson. It's more important to demonstrate how you teach than what the students will learn. For the demo lesson: *Keep it simple*!

Teaching Techniques

As for actually teaching the class, you already know you should be energetic, friendly, patient and professional. You should also keep some important teaching techniques in mind:

TEACHER/STUDENT TALKING RATIO. This is the amount of class time you spend talking compared to the amount of time the students talk. Remember, you already know how to speak English; the students are the ones who need to practice. A good rule of thumb is to maintain a 30/70 ratio. As the teacher you should only speak 30 percent of the time (a difficult feat for the rookie *sensei* to master).

COMMUNICATING WITH YOUR STUDENTS. Speak clearly and slowly, and project your voice so that everyone can hear. In this sample demo lesson the students are beginners so they may have a difficult time understanding you in the first class. Use the blackboard as much as possible. Put your name, the lesson objective and an outline of the lesson plan on the board. Whenever you have trouble communicating, write the words on the board.

When communicating verbally use just a few words if necessary. For example, if you want a student to stand up, just say "please stand up" and use a hand gesture. If you want students to repeat something as a class, point to all of them, say "please repeat" and then put your hand to your ear as if to listen.

MODELING. Modeling is another communication technique to use in the classroom. You model what you want the students to do by physically showing the students. For example, you will probably have to model making the nameplates. You will also model the role-playing by writing "famous people" on the board and having a student ask you the questions. Then introduce yourself as some outrageous famous person.

PROMPTING. Prompting is another good tool. If you want a student to say something, give him/her the first word, or point to a sentence written on the board and say "please say" to prompt a student to respond.

Finally, be subtle with your corrections and generous with your praise. Correct the students during specific parts of the lesson, for example during the main lesson, but let them go during the activity. And always praise the students when they make an effort, regardless of whether they are successful or not. Make the students feel good and have fun!

9

Choosing an Employer

What to Look For

Many job seekers don't appreciate that the interview process is a two-way street. Starting with the first phone call, the school is sizing you up, and you should be doing the same with them. Make a thorough evaluation of the potential employer before you make a committment. When you're ready to sign a contract, you want to be confident you have chosen a good school to work for.

The First Phone Conversation

Your evaluation begins with your first phone call to the school. In the beginning you may be a little naive about what to look for. After a couple of telephone calls and in-person interviews, you'll wise up quickly.

Over the phone you can determine a lot about the school by listening. Does the person on the phone speak understandable English? If not, this could be a problem.

This may be a small office that can't afford support staff with English-speaking ability. The person on the phone may be the person you would have to rely on for assistance if you work for this school. If you can't communicate, life could be difficult.

Did you talk to at least two people? This shows they are professional enough to at least appear as though they have a receptionist. The personality of the person you are talking with should tell you something. The school chose this person to make a first impression.

When you are invited for an interview, evaluate the directions they give. Are they clear and concise? Are you or the other person confused? This could be a sign of things to come.

At the School

The school and its location are important. The in-house school should be a place in which you would enjoy teaching every day. For an in-company school, determine if the office seems professional. Does it have space for you to prepare lesson plans? What is the neighborhood like? Is the school or office conveniently located near a subway/train station? Would you feel safe leaving the school at 10 p.m.?

The Interview

In the previous chapter I pointed out that the interview is an opportunity for you to convince the school that you're the best person for the job. It is also the time when you should find out if this is the best school for you.

QUESTIONS TO ASK. The following are the basic questions you should ask. Get as much information as you can during your initial phone conversation, before you invest time and money attending an in-person interview. You absolutely must ask all of these questions before signing a contract:

- *What is the salary range?* Get this information in the first phone call, but ask this question in a subtle way. If the salary isn't in your desired range you shouldn't waste a trip to their office.

- *How many hours of work a week?* The school will require a minimum number of teaching hours a week for the guaranteed salary. Ask how many other non-teaching hours you must work. These could include office hours and testing.

- *What type of teaching?* Is it in-house, company or another type? For in-house schools, what type of students (children, students, adults)?

- *How many hours a week traveling?* (For in-company schools). This is another requirement of your time that doesn't fall under teaching, office hours or testing. Some in-company teachers travel more than three hours a day to classes. Ask if they compensate for travel time.

- *When would you be working?* What days and times must you be available for work? Working on Saturday is common; Sunday isn't. Schools will usually require you to be available to work certain hours of the day, for example, from 9 a.m. to 9 p.m. Being available to work doesn't mean you'll actually work those hours. What hours will you usually work?

- *What is the school's training program like?* Training programs range from professionally prepared 20-hour intensive programs to the owner of the school handing you a book and showing you the classroom. Determine what your training needs are. Do you feel you need a lot of training or could you start teaching with very little training?

• *How long has the school been in business?* Scrutinize recent start-ups. A few fly-by-night operations try to take advantage of the billion dollar English conversation industry—and teachers' paychecks.

• *How many teachers do they have?* The number of teachers tells you how big the school is. You shouldn't decide what school to work for solely on the basis of its size, but it is something you should take into account. Among the national chains there are both great schools and horrible schools to work for. Even among the different branches of a national chain, working conditions vary. Working conditions at small schools definitely vary. A mom-and-pop English conversation school may be the best place to be taken care of, or it could be the worst place to be taken advantage of.

• *How many schools or branch offices?* This is another indication of size; it's also beneficial if you want to work in another part of Japan.

Get as much of this information over the phone as possible. Be sure you get all of the above information before signing a contract. Be subtle with your questions. Your goal is to get hired. Don't turn the interviewer off by grilling her/him.

The answers to these questions will be important in your evaluation. The following actions will also be important:

MEET YOUR BOSS. Make sure you meet the person who will be your direct supervisor before you sign a contract. Few things in life are more miserable than working for somebody you don't respect or get along with.

MEET THE STAFF. Try to meet as many of the support staff and management as possible. The support staff will be important to you for everything from your paycheck to getting your everyday life in Japan in order. Make sure that at least one member of the Japanese staff speaks adequate English.

In addition to your direct supervisor, try to meet other managers. Management sets the tone for the school. If you don't meet them, at least get the inside scoop from the teachers.

MEET THE TEACHERS. Do not sign a contract without talking to the teachers with whom you'll be working. If you aren't allowed to talk to them, don't work for this school. The school is hiding something. The best place to talk with the teachers is in the teachers' lounge, away from the bosses. Better yet, find out where they go after work and meet them there.

READ THE TEACHERS' POLICY. The teachers' policy should be written. It should cover every detail of your association with the school and your responsibilities as a teacher. Look for the following in the policy:

- *Teacher responsibilities*. What days and hours must you be available for teaching assignments, office hours, testing and other requirements? What meetings and training sessions are you required to attend? What reports are required and how often must you submit them?
- *Dress standards*. Most policies say your appearance should be, "business-like, neat and conservative." Watch out if the dress code gets too picky.
- *Socializing with students*. Some schools forbid any contact with students outside of class, while others

encourage it. Dating your students isn't a good idea, regardless of the policy.

- *Termination of contract*. Find out what reasons the school can use to fire you, and how you can terminate the contract in good standing.

Go over the policy carefully. Clarify anything you don't understand. Some schools have 20-page documents regulating your every move in Japan. Others may not have any written policies. Be wary of both extremes.

Use all the information you have gathered, from the first phone call to the teachers' policy, to evaluate the school. Consider everything. Decide if the school meets your needs.

One final but critical factor to consider before making your decision is the compensation package. The next chapter provides information about what to look for in compensation packages.

10

Compensation

Get the Best Deal

The compensation package is an important element in your evaluation of a school as a potential employer. In this adventure you have to make a living. Evaluate the compensation package thoroughly before you sign a contract.

The purpose of this chapter is to give you an idea what to consider when you evaluate the compensation package. This information is primarily intended for job-seekers considering work at the language schools. Compensation and teaching hours in traditional schools are structured differently. *Sensei* who work for a university should earn a higher salary than teachers in the language schools. If you are considering a university or another traditional teaching position, calculate the hourly pay rate and decide if it is fair. The Appendix has examples of compensation packages from large, medium and small language schools.

The Compensation Package

Below is an outline of the compensation package offered by a large, multi-branch in-company school, followed by an explanation of each element of the package.

Guaranteed monthly salary: ¥250,000 ($2,273). Based on a minimum of 20 hours teaching a week.

After minimum pay rate (overtime pay rate): ¥3,000 ($27) to ¥4,000 ($36) an hour.

Sick leave: Six sick days a year and a long-term disability plan.

Vacation & holidays: Five vacation days after completing the first year. All national holidays are paid. One week off at Christmas and one week in August are not paid.

Health insurance: Private health insurance is provided.

Transportation expenses: Reimbursed (from home to class and back).

Completion bonus: ¥100,000 ($909) paid upon completion of one year contract.

Apartment: School provides apartment, pays key money and deposits. Employee pays rent.

Second year raise: ¥10,000 ($91) to ¥20,000 ($182) a month; second year completion bonus ¥120,000 ($1,090).

Term of contract: One year.

Example Compensation Package

GUARANTEED MONTHLY SALARY. This is the minimum monthly salary the school pays on the basis of a specified number of minimum hours worked. This example contract specifies 20 hours a week as the minimum. If the school actually assigns only 19 hours or less, you will still receive full salary.

The minimum number of hours varies from school to school. It ranges from 20 to 40 hours per week, with most schools requiring about 25 to 30 hours. Ask about other demands on your time. For example, does the school require you to work office hours or do testing? If so, do they pay you for this extra work? Regardless of whether or not the school requires you to work office hours, you have to plan to spend time preparing your lesson plans. In the beginning it will take longer, perhaps as much as an hour of preparation per hour of teaching. But as you gain experience your preparation time should decrease.

You can use the following calculation to determine the average hourly rate offered by a school: divide the monthly guaranteed salary (MGS) by the total number of hours (TNH) you must work to determine the hourly pay rate (HPR):

$$\text{MGS} \div \text{TNH} = \text{HPR}$$

Working hours should include teaching hours, office hours, testing and travel time in excess of two hours a day. Some schools compensate separately for testing and excessive travel time; if so, don't include them in the calculation.

AFTER-MINIMUM PAY RATE. This is the hourly rate schools pay for work after you satisfy the required minimum hours. We call it overtime pay. This school paid ¥3,000 ($27) an hour for day classes and ¥4,000 ($36) for evening classes. The traditional schools probably won't have a pay structure like this; their teachers generally work a 40-hour week for a specific salary.

Determine when overtime pay starts. If the contract requires 20 minimum hours, do you get overtime for the 21st hour in a week, even though you worked less than 80 hours for the month (20 hours x 4 weeks = 80 hours)? Or do you have to work 80 hours before receiving the higher rate?

Find out how many hours over the minimum you can expect to work. This is where you make the big money. Some schools may indicate that a lot of overtime work is involved in order to entice you. To get an accurate idea ask the teachers how many overtime hours they work. If there is little overtime, you can always make extra income through part-time and private work.

SICK LEAVE. This school provides six sick days a year and a long-term disability plan. Be sure you understand the sick leave policy. People get a lot of colds in Japan.

VACATION. Few English language schools offer paid vacation days during the first year, so paid holidays are important to you as a rookie teacher. As hard as the Japanese supposedly work they have a lot of national holidays. In addition to these holidays the whole country takes about a week's vacation three times a year. Teachers at the traditional high schools and universities have a definite advantage because they enjoy the same vacations as the students. But make sure that they're paid vacations.

At the language schools determine which holidays the school observes and if they're paid. Also ask what their policy is on the New Year's, Golden Week and O-Bon holidays; how much time do they take off, and is it paid?

HEALTH INSURANCE. Japan's reasonably priced national health insurance is available to you after you become employed. Schools pay either all or part of your national or private health insurance. If it is private insurance, ask about the details; the policy probably has limits and deductibles.

TRANSPORTATION. All schools should pay the cost of your round-trip transportation from your front door to the classroom. Find out if they reimburse for direct costs or simply give you an allowance. If it's an allowance, make sure it's enough to cover your transportation expenses.

COMPLETION BONUS. This school gives a bonus when you finish your contract. The bonus gives you an incentive to stay for the duration of your contract. If the contract is for one year, the school will pay the bonus exactly at the end of one year—not one day sooner. Some schools may offer to pay your air fare home or a similar gimmick as a bonus. You must decide if the bonus is fair. Pay attention.

APARTMENT ASSISTANCE. This school provides an apartment for each of its teachers. The school also pays deposits and key money (key money is a non-refundable deposit that must be paid to the landlord and real estate agent; this is sometimes as much as four times the monthly rent). The teacher only pays the rent and utilities.

Most schools that hire full-time teachers should offer some kind of apartment assistance, such as:

- The school provides an apartment and pays the key money.
- The school pays the key money.
- Utopia. The school provides an apartment, pays all the key money and the rent. Pinch yourself, you're dreaming (sometimes dreams come true).

At the very least, the school should offer a low-interest loan to cover the key money and set-up costs. They should also help you find an apartment.

If the school leaves you on your own, you will survive. Many *gaijin* have done it before you. It just makes your life easier if the school helps you in some way.

SECOND YEAR RAISE. This school gives its teachers an automatic raise of ¥10,000 ($91) per month starting the 13th month. Teachers also receive an additional tax-free monthly bonus of up to ¥10,000 ($91) on the basis of their previous year's performance. This school wants to keep their quality teachers.

Schools should provide incentives to stay longer than the original contract. If the school doesn't offer a significant raise or contract renewal bonus, it isn't serious about having quality teachers; it's more interested in getting a body into the classroom at the lowest cost.

OTHER BENEFITS. Benefits vary from school to school. Health club membership, a company car, installation of a phone and free Japanese lessons have all been used as enticements. A few schools (very few) offer to pay the cost of your trip to Korea to obtain your work visa. The perks can be unusual sometimes, depending on what business the school owner's brother-in-law is in.

CONSIDER THE ENTIRE PACKAGE. You should consider the package as a whole. For example, if a school is offering a lower salary but will pay for your rent, the installation of your telephone, or some other such compensation, determine the value of all non-monetary benefits and weigh them against the decreased salary. Make a chart listing the salary, hourly pay rate and all the other benefits for each school offering you a job and compare them.

Cost of Living in Tokyo vs. Other Cities

Another consideration when evaluating a compensation package is where you will be living and working. Tokyo is the most expensive city in Japan. In smaller cities or rural areas, the cost of living can be considerably less. The major difference will be the cost of housing. In Tokyo ¥50,000 ($455) a month may get you a room in a *gaijin* house, while in Fukuoka (a major city on the southern island of Kyushu) you can rent a small apartment for the same price.

Another good cost-of-living barometer is the price of a bowl of udon. At a Tokyo train station it costs about ¥350 ($3), at a Fukuoka station it costs ¥250 ($2.25).

Most schools take the cost of living into consideration when setting salaries. Salaries in Tokyo should be at least ¥10,000 ($91) a month higher than other areas, although some schools in the outlying areas may match the Tokyo salaries to entice teachers. A salary of ¥250,000 ($2,273) a month will go farther outside of Tokyo, in some places a lot farther.

Taxes and Health Insurance

The Japanese government takes only about 5 to 10 percent of your paycheck, a very reasonable tax rate. The government also assesses a 3 percent consumption (sales) tax on items purchased. Your country may want some of your foreign salary, too. For example, citizens of the United States must pay taxes on foreign earnings over $70,000 a year. If you make that much you can afford to pay some taxes. Check with your country's tax agency to determine if you need to file a return or pay taxes on your foreign earnings.

The cost of your national health insurance is based on your previous year's salary. For *gaijin* teachers this means your first year's cost will be low (you had no salary last year) but it will go up in future years. Health insurance costs vary from city to city. Even within the same city the cost sometimes varies from teacher to teacher. Confusion seems to be the rule for health insurance costs. Sometimes the price is negotiable.

If the school does not include health insurance or requires you to pay all or some of the premium determine the cost of the insurance. Ask the school what you can expect to pay. Also ask some of the teachers what they are currently paying.

11

The Work Visa

Don't Sweat it

The anticipation of obtaining a work visa causes some prospective English conversation *sensei* the most anxiety of their entire Japan adventure. Obtaining a work visa is something you should be aware of, but don't be anxious about it. You just concentrate on getting a job—let the school that hires you (and becomes your sponsor) worry about your work visa.

The Mind-Boggling Facts

The following are some mind-boggling facts about the work visa. Visas (which allow you to stay in the country) are only issued *outside* of Japan. If you are lucky enough to get hired outside of Japan, you will be issued a work visa at the Japanese Embassy or Consulate before you leave for Japan. If you are hired *within* Japan you must *leave* Japan and go to a Japanese Embassy or Consulate in a foreign country to apply for and receive your work visa (e.g. Korea).

VISA EXEMPTION. Citizens of most English-speaking countries are allowed to enter Japan as tourists under a visa exemption arrangement. This allows you to enter Japan with only a valid passport (you don't need to obtain a visa prior to leaving your country). When you enter Japan, Immigration stamps "90-Day Visitor Status" into your passport. This is your visa exemption.

It is the current practice of the Japanese government not to issue U.S. citizens a tourist visa. If you could obtain a tourist visa you could simply change your visa status from tourist to work visa after you were hired/sponsored by a school, without leaving Japan. Unfortunately at this time this is not an option, but before you leave for Japan see if you can obtain a tourist visa.

THE PATH TO YOUR WORK VISA. After you enter Japan under a "Visitor Status" visa exemption, the path to your work visa goes like this:

1. The school that hires you becomes your sponsor and processes all the paperwork you need to obtain your work visa. You must provide the school with your passport, a resume and certificate of graduation (diploma).

2. When the paperwork is ready you must take it to a Japanese Embassy or Consulate (these are located outside of Japan). Along with the paperwork, you must submit two passport-size photos. The Embassy processes the paperwork and issues the visa. Officially, Japan Immigration says that it takes from one to eight weeks to process a work visa. All of the *sensei* I know were able to pick up their visa from the Japanese Embassy in Seoul, Korea, within 48 hours. Another *sensei* received his visa within 24 hours from the Consulate in San Francisco.

3. After you return to Japan with your work visa in hand, you must register with your local ward office and obtain your alien registration card (your sponsor will tell you where/how/when).

4. You make lots of yen and have a wonderful time.

Getting a work visa isn't that big a deal. If you get close to the end of your 90-day visa exemption you can always exit the country, take an overnight ferry ride to Korea, and then re-enter Japan for another 90 days. Some people do this as a way to work without a visa, but Japan Immigration catches on after a while.

LEAVING JAPAN TO OBTAIN A WORK VISA. As for leaving the country to get your work visa, most new *sensei* consider this a bonus adventure. It's a chance to see Korea, Hong Kong or Thailand. Most visa seekers head to Korea because it's the cheapest destination at about $175 to $200 by airplane. A ferry is cheaper; check your travel guide or ask the TIC. Another advantage of going to Korea is that the Japanese Embassy in Seoul is familiar with the process and usually issues the work visa within 48 hours.

If you go to a country other than Korea, try to determine in advance how long the Japanese Embassy there will take to issue the visa. You must pick up the visa in person. This could be a problem if it takes more than a couple of days.

Some time will elapse from the date the school hires you until the date you leave Japan to get your work visa (usually about a month). Most language schools will put new *sensei* to work right away, even though you don't have a work visa. When the paperwork for the work visa is ready you take a couple of days off to leave Japan and obtain it.

DON'T SWEAT IT. My advice about obtaining your work visa is: Don't sweat it. The school that hires you should do all the worrying. Before you leave for Japan get the latest visa information from the Embassy or Consulate. Circumstances change and you may find more favorable information.

Canadians, Australians and New Zealanders should ask about working holiday visas. A working holiday visa allows you to travel and work in Japan for six months with two additional six-month extensions (total of 18 months).

The Cultural Visa

Earlier I mentioned the cultural visa as a way to work without a university degree. This visa allows you to study some aspect of the Japanese culture and work for a certain number of hours a week. You can study anything from the language or martial arts to flower arranging.

I know of several *gaijin* who chose to study Japanese full-time at the YMCA (four hours a day) and then work full-time (two to four hours a day) with a cultural visa. The school you attend must be one that the government considers legitimate, and you are required to attend a certain number of hours a week. For more information, contact the Embassy or Consulate and ask for information about the cultural visa. Don't mention your desire to work.

12

Settling In

Congratulations!

You've done it! You traveled halfway around the world, survived on next to nothing and now you have a job. This book should be finished. The goal was to help you find a teaching position in Japan, and you succeeded. There is, however, some more you should know about your stay in Japan. This is information *gaijin* sometimes don't discover for months and sometimes never. This book doesn't intend to be an expert source on settling in. Your main sources of information will be your fellow teachers, the school's office staff and all of your Japanese friends.

Your fellow teachers are the best source for information because they have recently gone through what you are just starting. Don't hesitate to ask them for advice. Teachers of English conversation feel a unique bond among themselves. As the new kid on the block you should be in everybody's good graces. You will receive many offers of help. Take advantage of them while you can; the honeymoon won't last forever.

Your school should have at least one staff member whose job description includes "helping the new teacher." Be nice to this person. He/she will help you with everything from processing your visa to getting the *Japan Times* delivered to your door (if you don't mind paying more than a buck a day). A helpful and resourceful staff person who assists you is a definite bonus (and something you considered before accepting the job).

Your Japanese friends will be invaluable. After all, this is their country, and if anybody knows the ins and outs, they do. They will sincerely want to help you. You are a guest in their country, and they take the role of host very seriously. All they ask in return is your friendship.

The Apato (Ah-pa-toe: Apartment)

FINDING AN APARTMENT. If your school doesn't provide any apartment assistance, you'll need to find one on your own. Don't panic; many *gaijin* do this. The Kinokuniya Book Store in Tokyo has several books/magazines with information for the apartment hunter.

FURNISHINGS. If you don't get a furnished apartment (you probably won't) you could be looking at just four walls. Items you took for granted, such as lights, curtains and hot water, may not come with your apartment. Don't panic; you can find everything and cheaply . . . if you are patient.

Many *gaijin* have more furniture in their Japanese apartments than they had at home. For example, my apartment in Japan contained the following: a TV/VCR, stereo, dresser, wardrobe, couch that folded into a bed, beautiful desk/bookshelf combination, a new (almost) dining room table with matching chairs, refrigerator (not standard in Japanese apartments), washing machine, gas heater (heat usually isn't provided with the apartment), *kotatsu*, and all the other items one needs to live a comfortable life.

A *kotatsu* is a low-standing table you put your legs under while sitting on the floor. Between the table top and the frame is a blanket that creates a kind of tent over a heater attached to the bottom of the frame. You just hunker down and stick your legs under the table. Insulation is virtually non-existent in Japan and heating your entire *apato* could kill you financially. The *kotatsu* is an inexpensive, intimate way to stay warm.

All that for a total of about $450. Nothing was new. I purchased most of it from other teachers who were leaving Japan and some at secondhand stores; and friends donated a lot. I literally had wall-to-wall furniture at a great price.

Your fellow teachers will be a good source for finding furniture. Pay attention to their *sayonara* sales. Ask them where the good secondhand shops are. Find out when *gomi* (go-me: garbage) day is. Usually once a month they have "big" *gomi* day when the Japanese throw out large items. Check out the perfectly good appliances and furniture the Japanese throw away. Many proud *gaijin* have furnished their apartments by perusing the trash put out on the street.

Publicizing what you need is another good idea. Mention to your friends that you are looking for a heater. You might receive one from a Japanese friend whose Uncle Hiroshi just bought a new one and doesn't need the old heater. Don't expect it, but don't be surprised if it happens occasionally.

Save money by being patient. I started with very little furniture, and after two months I had just one chair to sit on. By the third month I had completely furnished my apartment. I went from barely functional to extremely comfortable in a short time and at very little expense. Patience is a virtue and a money saver.

You'll recoup most of your furniture costs when you leave Japan. You will have a *sayonara* sale that helps another new *sensei*.

TELEPHONE. Hold onto your wallet because this might scare you. Buying the rights to a phone line in Japan costs about ¥75,000 ($681). This is what it costs to have the phone company (NTT) install or activate the telephone line in your apartment (it is not a bad perk if your school offers to provide a phone as part of your compensation). You then own the rights to that phone line for the rest of eternity. Fortunately, *gaijin* teachers don't usually remain in *Nihon* for the rest of eternity. You can sell the rights to your phone when you leave.

You might be able to buy the rights to a phone line from a departing *sensei* for a discount of ¥5,000 ($45) to ¥10,000 yen ($91). If you do buy the rights from someone, handle the transaction at your local NTT office to make sure it's legitimately transferred to your name.

TELEVISION. When you can afford it, get a television. This is a great way to help you with your Japanese studies. It will also provide you with the same mind-numbing escape you received at home, and you can get some of the programs in English.

The Japanese have bilingual television. For example, when an American movie is on they dub it in Japanese. With a special tuner you can get the original sound in English. The newer televisions have the bilingual tuner built into them, but you probably won't be able to afford these. You will be able to afford a secondhand portable radio/cassette player; make sure it is equipped with the bilingual television frequency.

NEIGHBORS. When you move into an apartment, it's a Japanese custom that you give your neighbors a present. If it's a large complex, just your immediate neighbors will suffice. The Japanese give presents like a towel or cake. You, however, can give them one of your *o-miyage* from home. It really is the thought that counts. If you can't speak Japanese, have one of your new Japanese friends write a note introducing you as the new neighbor.

PAYING THE BILLS. There are three ways you can pay your gas, electricity and water bills: go to the department's office and pay in person; sit at home and wait for somebody to come to your door to collect; or have it automatically deducted from your bank account each month.

One *gaijin* didn't know about the bank option until shortly before his departure, and he insisted that I include this "incredible" convenience in this section. Bills are never mailed because the Japanese don't write checks. Japan is strictly a cash society. Ask your fellow *gaijin* and new Japanese friends what they recommend.

Money

BANKS. The banks operate a little differently from what you are used to. It takes a lot more time to make a transaction in a Japanese bank. For some reason, every transaction involves at least three employees. The whole process goes like this: (1) you walk in and take a number; (2) they call your number and it appears on a sign; (3) you go to the available window, hand the teller what you want transacted and then sit down again; (4) when they are ready, they call your name and you return to the window to complete the transaction. If words need to be spoken, they will find somebody who speaks English.

OPENING A BANK ACCOUNT. Your school will probably deposit your pay check directly into your bank account. The school usually chooses the bank, and they should help you open your account. A note from the school that includes all of the pertinent information (your address, tax number etc.) and explains that you want to open an account is all you need. Be sure to get an ATM card. You don't want to spend twenty minutes inside the bank just to get some spending money.

ATM. All the information on the screen is in Japanese. Don't panic. Either your school or the bank can explain how to use the ATM. Since your school will deposit your check directly into your account the only information you need is which button to push to make a withdrawal. If you don't get the information from the bank or the school, your friends can show you in a few minutes.

CREDIT CARDS. The more expensive places accept Visa and Mastercard. If you're on a tight budget you won't be frequenting the more expensive places, so you won't be using your credit card too often. If you need to get extra cash with your credit card only a few banks do this. Look for a Visa or Mastercard sign outside the bank. Sumitomo provides this service and has branches everywhere. Go to the foreign exchange counter.

SENDING MONEY HOME. If you need to send money home to pay bills or to save (Japanese interest rates are criminally low), there are several ways to do this. You can make a bank-to-bank transfer, but this can be complicated and expensive. You can also buy travelers checks in dollars and send them home. Or you can buy a money order at the Post Office and have it sent to your financial guardian at home. Unfortunately the person to whom it is addressed must go to the Post Office personally to receive the *cash* (not a check—it made my mother nervous to be handed a thousand dollars cash at the Post Office, so I began sending my monthly savings to my brother).

Ask your fellow teachers how they send their money home. Try to find an English-speaking banker to give you some advice. Compare the different options because cost varies and some are more convenient.

Miscellaneous

ALIEN REGISTRATION CARD. After you have your work visa you must get an alien registration card (more affectionately known as a *gaijin* card). Always carry it with you. It fits into your wallet and you don't need to carry your passport any longer. If a police officer asks to see it (which will probably never happen when you are carrying it) and you don't have it, you'll spend hours at the police station explaining why. Remember to apologize profusely.

RE-ENTRY PERMITS. After you have your work visa, if you want to take a trip out of Japan you must get a re-entry permit from Immigration. This allows you to re-enter Japan without changing your visa status. Ask your school for more details.

TAX REFUND. Before you leave Japan for good, stop by the tax office. They will probably owe you a tax refund.

NHK TV. This is a quasi-government television station, similar to America's PBS system. The difference is its source of funding. Instead of the familiar on-the-air fundraising programs, NHK sends somebody to your house to collect. This person will tell you to pay X amount of yen for the use of NHK. Tell this person you don't have a TV and do not pay her/him! You are not required to. This little extortion bothers not only the *gaijin* but also the Japanese.

Private and Part-Time Work

As you begin to settle in you will find that you have some free time. What better way to spend your free time than making some extra money?

THE BIG MONEY. Your guaranteed monthly salary will be only about ¥250,000 ($2,273) a month. You may be wondering how you can save $1,000 month on that salary. It would be difficult.

Remember that your guaranteed salary is based on only about 25 hours of teaching a week (this varies from school to school). If you work an additional 15 hours a week (60 hours a month) at a pay rate of ¥3,000 ($27) an hour, that's an additional ¥180,000 ($1,636) a month. There's your $1,000 monthly savings. The pay rate of ¥3,000 an hour used above is a little on the low side. Some *sensei* command as much as ¥10,000 ($91) an hour for private work, and ¥5,000 ($45) an hour is common for private and part-time work.

This is why it is important to know the minimum number of required teaching hours and other demands for your time. If two schools offer the same guaranteed salary, the one that has the lower minimum required teaching hours and demands on your time is providing the better hourly rate. Be sure to do the pay rate calculation recommended on page 119.

If your school doesn't offer much overtime work, you will still be able to make some additional income through part-time or private work. Part-time work means you work for another employer on a part-time basis. Private work means that you receive fees directly from your students. Private work can be more lucrative than part-time work.

PART-TIME WORK. Each Monday the *Japan Times* carries dozens of ads for part-time teachers. Hourly rates will range from ¥2,000 ($18) to ¥5,000 ($45). An even better source for part-time work will be your network. Fellow teachers and friends who have been around for a while know where the choice jobs are. In the beginning you will be working at the lower end of the pay scale while you learn the secrets of the trade.

Don't alienate your sponsor (the school that employs you full-time). They'll probably have something in the contract or teachers' policy that deals with moonlighting. It may specifically state you are not allowed to work anywhere else. What is written and what is reality sometimes differs. Ask your fellow teachers about the school's "unofficial policy."

It's a good idea not to work for a direct competitor of your sponsoring school and to keep all other moonlighting very low key. One Canadian *sensei* was fired from his full-time job when his school saw his photograph in an advertisement for another English conversation school where he was working part-time. He lost both jobs. Your sponsor always comes first.

PRIVATE WORK. Private work can be more profitable but it takes more effort on your part. In the larger cities, where large numbers of *gaijin* congregate, private work may be harder to find. It's simple supply and demand. In some out-of-the-way cities or remote areas of Japan, many *sensei* clean up.

There are two ways to get private work. Other teachers might give you their private work because they are leaving or just don't have time for these students. Or you can get private students on your own. This means you have to meet potential students.

Get out and about as much as possible, especially in the beginning. The more you circulate, the more people you will meet and the more opportunities for additional income. Going out a lot may be expensive at first, but you must consider it another investment.

Business cards are to Japanese as air is to life. Your school will give you business cards with their logo and phone number on it, but you want to hand out your own card, which indicates you're available for private work. Put your phone number on the cards but not your address.

ONE TEACHER'S GOLD MINE. To give you an idea of how moonlighting can pay off, the following is the schedule of a *sensei* who worked full-time (20 to 25 hours a week) for a company school in a city of one million people (not Tokyo, Osaka, Hiroshima, or Kyoto, the most popular *gaijin* destinations).

His part-time work included five hours a week at a small school that taught all ages in small groups (one to four people). It paid him ¥5,000 ($45) an hour. One morning a week he taught at a junior college that paid him ¥18,000 ($163) for three hours of teaching. He also had part-time work at two YMCA schools.

His private work included two children's classes, ages five to nine years; two classes with high school students; and four classes for adults. The children's classes were held early Saturday afternoon and the adult's classes were all after he finished his evening classes for his sponsoring school.

His part-time and private work totaled 14 to 16 hours a week, and he received ¥5,000 ($45) an hour. All of that work added up to over ¥70,000 ($630) a week, or ¥280,000 ($2,730) a month in additional income. Add to this his guaranteed salary of ¥250,000 ($2,273), and he was making over ¥530,000 ($4,818) a month. He was able to live very well on less than ¥250,000 ($2,273) a month and saved the rest. You can see how, with just a little effort on your part, you can significantly increase your income. *Gambatte!*

Culture Shock

Finally, a few words about culture shock. No matter how much reading you have done or how many first-hand accounts of life in Japan you have heard, you will still experience culture shock. Many authors write about the different stages of adapting to life in a new culture. I didn't pay attention when I read about these stages. But as I look back on my letters home and the journal that I kept, I see that I went through similar stages.

It begins with the *Wonderment* stage. Here you have arrived in a city of more than 12 million people to begin your adventure. Everything is new, exciting, and—well, wonderful. You have a very positive feeling about your adventure and everything you encounter in Japan is seen in that positive light. My wonderment stage continued until after I was employed and had moved into my new city and employment.

By about the second month I began what I call the *Entering-reality* stage, when the newness wears off and you must start to deal with the day-to-day realities of your new life. You have to learn how to deal with the post office, the banks and every other aspect of the daily working person's life. It still has a positive spin to it, but reality is creeping in.

I specifically remember identifying the next stage. I call it the *What-the-hell-is-with-this-place?* stage. Late one night I was in a bar throwing back whiskeys and complaining about everything. A good friend of mine who had a year of experience in Japan was sitting with me, trying to keep up with my whiskeys and letting me go on with my complaints. He finally stopped me and asked, "How long have you been here?" After thinking about it, I told him, "It'll be six months next week."

"That's it!" he responded. I had hit the six-month stage. The newness and wonderment of it all had worn off, and I was now trying to cope with the strains of living in a foreign culture. He said it had happened to him at exactly the same time.

He correctly predicted that it would pass during the coming weeks and told me that to be successful, I would learn to deal with the negatives and exploit the positives. I identify this as the *Learning-to-deal-with-it* stage. This was the way I finished my final year. I took advantage of the many perks a *gaijin* teacher can enjoy and laughed at the frustrating aspects of living in a foreign culture.

These stages occur at different times for different *gaijin*. I know some who have never left the wonderment stage (I worry about these people) and other *gaijin* who hit the "What-the-hell-is-with-this-place?" stage within a month. These latter *gaijin* don't have that adventuresome spirit. They don't have the patience or flexibility to deal with the way things differ in a foreign country, and they definitely don't have a sense of humor. I hope that your wonderment phase is long-lasting, that your third stage is brief and painless and that your entire experience is a success.

Appendix

Japan National Tourist Organization

Contact a JNTO office and ask for the information listed on page 48.

United States

630 5th Ave.
New York, NY 10111
Phone: (212) 757-5640

401 N. Michigan Ave., Ste. 770
Chicago, IL 60611
Phone: (312) 222-0874

2121 San Jacinto St., Ste. 980
Dallas, TX 75201
Phone: (214) 754-1820

360 Post St., Ste. 401
San Francisco, CA 94108
Phone: (415) 989-7140

624 S. Grand Ave., Ste. 1611
Los Angeles, CA 90017
Phone: (213) 623-1952

Canada

165 University Ave.
Toronto, Ontario M5H 3B8
Phone: (416) 366-7140

United Kingdom

167 Regent St.
London W1
Phone: (01) 734-9638

Australia

115 Pitt St.
Sydney NSW 2000
Phone: (02) 232-4522

Youth Hostel Information

American Youth Hostels, Inc
P.O. Box 37613
Washington, DC 20013

Contact a nearby International Youth Hostel or American Youth Hostels to obtain a card.

Japan Youth Hostels Inc.
Hoken Kaikan
1-2 Sadohara-cho
Ichigaya, Shinjuku-ku
Tokyo 162
Japan
Phone: 03/3269-5831

Contact JYH for information and a map of hostels in Japan.

Tokyo Intl. Youth Hostel
Central Plaza Bld. 18F
21-1 Kagura-gashi
Shinjuku-ku
Tokyo 162
Japan
Phone: 03/3235-1107

On page 76 I suggest Tokyo International Youth Hostel as a place to stay your first few nights. Make reservations by sending two international reply coupons.

Japanese Book Stores

The following book stores stock thousands of books about Japan including those listed in Chapter 4, "Preparing to Go." They also stock books written in Japanese. They accept phone orders and can provide a list of popular books about Japan.

Kinokuniya Book Stores

1581 Webster St.
San Francisco, CA 94115
Phone: (415) 567-7625

675 Saratoga Ave.
San Jose, CA 95129
Phone: (408) 252-1300

123 Astronaut Ellison Onizuka
Los Angeles, CA 90012
Phone: (213) 687-4480

2141 West 182nd St.
Torrance, CA 90504
Phone: (310) 327-6577

665 Paularino Ave.
Costa Mesa, CA 92626
Phone: (714) 434-9986

519 6th Ave. South
Seattle, WA 98104
Phone: (206) 587-2477

10 West 49th St.
New York, NY 10020
Phone: (212) 765-1461

595 River Rd.
Edgewater, NJ 07020
Phone: (201) 941-7580

Asahiya Book Stores

Little Tokyo Square
333 S. Alameda St. #108
Los Angeles, CA 90013
Phone: (213) 626-5650

4240 Kerny Mesa Rd.
St. #119-128
San Diego, CA 92111
Phone: (619) 565-0100

100 E. Algonquin Rd. #106
Arlington Heights, IL 60005
Phone: (708) 228-9851

52 Vanderbilt
New York, NY 10017
Phone: (212) 883-0011

Sasuga

7 Upland Rd.
Cambridge, MA 02140
Phone: (617) 497-5460

Anzen Pacific

7750 N.E. 17th Ave.
Portland, OR 97211
Phone: (503) 283-1284

Japanese Embassies and Consulates

1. *Visa Information. Ask the Embassy or Consulate near you for written information about the work or cultural visa. Ask for the booklet titled "Visa Information (Visa Application Procedures for Entry into Japan)." Ask if it is possible to obtain a tourist or working holiday visa.*
2. *Write to receive information and an application for the JET Program (applications are usually sent out in early October).*
3. *The Embassy and Consulates have libraries open to the public. Ask if they have the* Japan Times *daily.*

Note: CGJ = Consulate General of Japan

Embassy of Japan
2520 Massachusetts Ave. NW
Washington, DC 20008
Phone: (202) 939-6800

Consulate Offices in U.S.

CGJ in Boston
Federal Reserve Plaza, 14F
600 Atlantic Ave.
Boston, MA 02210
Phone: (617) 973-9772

CGJ in New York
299 Park Ave.
New York, NY 10171
Phone: (212) 371-8222

CGJ in Atlanta
100 Colony Square #2000
1175 Peach Tree St., N.E.
Atlanta, GA 30361
Phone: (404) 892-5067

CGJ in New Orleans
One Poydras Plaza, Ste. 2050
639 Loyola Ave.
New Orleans, LA 70113
Phone: (504) 529-2101

CGJ in Chicago
Olympia Center, Ste. 1000
737 North Michigan Ave.
Chicago, IL 60611
Phone: (312) 280-0430

CGJ in Kansas City
2519 Commerce Tower
911 Main St.
Kansas City, MO 64105
Phone: (816) 471-0111

CGJ in Houston
First Interstate Plaza, Ste. 5300
1000 Louisiana St.
Houston, TX 77002
Phone: (713) 652-2977

CGJ in Los Angeles
350 South Grand Ave.
Los Angeles, CA 90071
Phone: (213) 624-8305

CGJ in San Francisco
50 Fremont St., Ste. 2200
San Francisco, CA 94105
Phone: (415) 777-3533

CGJ in Portland
2400 First Interstate Tower
1300 S.W. 5th Ave.
Portland, OR 97201
Phone: (503) 221-1811

CGJ in Seattle
601 Union St., Ste. 500
Seattle, WA 98101
Phone: (206) 224-4374

CGJ in Anchorage
550 West 7th Ave., Ste. 701
Anchorage, AK 99501
Phone: (907) 279-8428

CGJ in Honolulu
1742 Nuuanu Ave.
Honolulu, HI 96817
Phone: (808) 536-2226

CGJ in Miami
World Trade Center, Ste. 3200
80 S.W. 8th St.
Miami, FL 33130
Phone: (305) 530-9090

Canada

Embassy of Japan
255 Sussex Drive
Ottawa, Ontario K1N 9E6
Phone: (613) 236-8541

CGJ in Montreal
600 Rue de Lagauchetiere Ouest
#1785
Montreal, Quebec H3B 4L8
Phone: (514) 866-3429

CGJ in Toronto
Dominion Center #1803
Toronto, Ontario M5K 1A1
Phone: (416) 363-7038

CGJ in Vancouver
1210-1177 W. Hastings St.
Vancouver, B.C. V6E 2K9
Phone: (604) 684-5868

CGJ in Edmonton
10020 100th St.
Edmunton, Alberta T5J 0N4
(403) 422-3752

CGJ in Winnipeg
730-215 Garry St.
Credit Union Center Plaza
Winnipeg, Manitoba R3C 3P3
Phone: (204) 943-5554

United Kingdom

Embassy of Japan
43-46 Grosvenor St.
London W1X 0BA
Phone: (01) 493-6030

Australia

Embassy of Japan
112 Empire Circuit
Yarralumla, Canberra
ACT 2600
Phone: (06) 273-3244

New Zealand

Embassy of Japan
Norwich Insurance House 7F
3-11 Hunter St.
Wellington 1
Phone: (04) 473-1540

TEFL Training Centers

For a complete list of schools throughout the world that offer the internationally recognized Certificate in the Teaching of English as a Foreign Language to Adults Program (CTEFLA), contact the University of Cambridge listed below or a British Council office in your country. I have listed the schools in North America, Australia and Japan that offer the certificate.

The Publications Department
The University of Cambridge
Local Examinations Syndicate
1 Hills Road
Cambridge CB1 2EU
United Kingdom

North America

Center for English Studies
450 Sansome St.
San Francisco, CA 94111
Phone (415) 986-0898

St. Giles Language Center
One Hallidie Plaza, Ste. 350
San Francisco, CA 94102
Phone: (415) 788-3552

Center for English Studies
330 7th Ave.
New York, NY 10001
Phone: (212) 620-0760

Coast Language Academy
20720 Ventura Bld., Ste. 300
Woodland Hills, CA 91364
Phone: (818) 346-5113

Australia

St. Marks International College
P.O. Box 8480
Stirling Street
Perth WA 6849
Phone: (619) 227-9888

Australian TESOL Training
P.O. Box 82
Bondi Junction
NSW 2022
Phone: (612) 389-0249

Japan

International Language Centre
Iwanami Jimbocho Bld. 9F
2-1 Kanda Jimbocho
Chiyoda-ku
Tokyo 101
Phone: 03/3264-5935

Job Hunting from North America

Contact these organizations when you begin your job search in North America. In some cases it may take several weeks for a response.

AEON
9301 Wilshire Blvd., Ste 202
Beverly Hills, CA 90210
Phone: (310) 550-0940

AEON is one of the largest multi-branch schools and does a lot of recruiting in North America. Write and ask when they will be recruiting. Include a resume.

Sony Language Laboratories
9 West 57th St.
New York, NY 10019
Phone: (212) 371-5800

Sony is a large multi-branch language school that recruits in North America. Write and ask when they will be recruiting.

YMCA of the USA
International Office for Asia
909 4th Ave.
Seattle, WA 98104
Phone: (206) 382-5008

YMCA has hundreds of language schools throughout Japan. This office places about 55 people from North America in teaching positions in Japan and Taiwan.

Geos
Box 12165 #419
808 Nelson St.
Vancouver, B.C. V6Z 2H2
Canada
Phone: (604) 684-5663

Geos
2312 Simpson's Tower
401 Bay St.
Toronto, Ontario M5H 2Y4
Canada
Phone: (416) 777-0109

Geos is a multi-branch language school. Write to the office closest to you for recruiting information. Include a resume.

IES
Shin Taiso Bld.
2-10-7 Dogenzaka
Shibuya-ku
Tokyo 150
Japan
Phone: 03/3463-5396

IES occasionally recruits in North America. A letter with a resume will probably get a response.

Interac
Foreign Recruiting Dept.
Fujibo Bld. 2F
2-10-28 Fujimi
Chiyoda-ku
Tokyo 102
Japan
Phone: 03/3234-7841

Interac is a large multi-branch school in Japan that periodically recruits in North America. A letter with a resume will probably get a response

Teachers of Speakers of
Other Languages, Inc. (TESOL)
1600 Cameron St. #300
Alexandria, VA 22314
Phone: (703) 836-0774

Ask TESOL for general information about their organization. Among their many publications, the Placement Bulletin *is the most valuable for the job hunter.*

Japan Association of Language
Teachers (JALT)
Shamboru Dai-2 Kawasaki #305
1-3-17 Kaizuka
Kawasaki-ku
Kawasaki 210
Japan

A cousin of TESOL in Japan, JALT also publishes a newsletter. They take a long time to respond.

Friends of World Teaching
PO Box 1049
San Diego, CA 92112
Phone: (619) 275-4066

For a about $20 you choose three countries and Friends will send a list of schools with ESL programs.

Council on International
Education Exchange (CIEE)
205 East 42nd St.
New York, NY 10017
Phone: (212) 661-1414

CIEE specializes in student travel, and work/study programs abroad. They have locations throughout the U.S. and Britain. Ask about the International Teacher card, low cost travel information and their publication Student Travel.

The Pacific Rim Advantage
702 Mangrove Ave. #165 1F
Chico, CA 95926

The Pacific Rim Advantage offers current lists of schools in Japan that are hiring EFL teachers. They also sell books and reports on teaching in Japan and about Japan in general.

The Japan Times

In North America you can order copies of the Japan Times *from two companies. Remember to ask for the Monday edition if you want the help wanted ads.*

Japan Times Weekly
3151 Airway Ave., # K105
Costa Mesa, CA 92626
Phone: (714) 549-2555
Toll Free: (800) 446-0200
Fax: (714) 549-2888

OCS America
1684 Post St.
San Francisco, CA 94115
Phone: (415) 931-0396
Fax: (415) 931-6728

Survey of Japan Times Help Wanted Ads

The following is a survey of the ads for English teachers that appeared in the Japan Times *Monday edition from October 1991 to January 1993. This gives you an idea of the recent job market for English teachers and what months have the most ads. The* Japan Times *has two want ad headings: "Female Only" and "Male & Female." I also tallied ads for part-time positions. Many ads were seeking more than one teacher; in those cases I counted the ad only, not the number of positions available. Consequently, the total number of available positions is always higher than the total of ads in each month.*

Date	Female Only	Male & Female	Part-time Positions
October 1991	15	32	46
November[1]	09	30	26
December[2]	11	30	21
January 1992	20	61	35
February	29	72	46
March*	25	60	78
April	25	57	63
May[3]	18	68	42
June*	69	118	61
July	28	70	61
August*	33	64	75
September	28	39	59
October	18	53	38
November*	16	48	35
December[4]	14	26	14
January 1993*	28	64	34

*These months had five Mondays.

[1] The 11/04 issue had only 2 ads for full-time positions. This date coincides with the Culture Day Holiday.

[2] The 12/23 issue had only 1 ad for a full-time position. This date falls within the Christmas holidays

[3] The 05/04 issue had no teacher help wanted ads. This date falls within the Golden Week holidays.

[4] The 12/21 and 12/28 issues had a combined total of 6 help wanted ads. These dates fall within the Christmas holidays.

Sample Compensation Packages

The following are highlights of compensation packages from four different schools: the YMCA, Japan American Club (a medium-size school), a large multi-branch company school (name withheld by request) and a small two-teacher school (name withheld by request). These packages were offered to new teachers in 1993.

Most schools have a contract and teachers' policy that go into greater detail than the highlights I have provided here. Following the highlights of the compensation packages, I have reproduced verbatim the contracts of the large and small school used in this section to give you an idea of how contracts look and vary. Please note that these are sample packages only. The salary figures will change, depending on the current market .

YMCA

The following information was provided by the YMCA's International Office for Asia, which is located in Seattle, Washington. This is a summary of the package that was offered to teachers who were hired in 1993. Note that individual YMCA schools throughout Japan may offer different compensation packages.

Salary: With a B.A., ¥250,000 to ¥280,000/month. With an M.A., ¥280,000 to ¥310,000/month. Salary depends on your applicable experience and the location of the school. Salaries for schools in Tokyo are higher.

Hours: 22 hours teaching and 18 office hours a week.

Health Insurance: Employer and employee share costs.

Housing: YMCA assists in finding an apartment. YMCA pays key money and deposits, employee pays rent. YMCA provides bed, lights, range, washing machine, refrigerator, heater/fan.

Transportation Expenses: Reimburses for transportation expenses between your home and the school.

Vacation: Minimum 25 working days paid vacation.

Bonus: Round-trip air fare from North America to Japan.

Other Benefits: Free Japanese language lessons.

Japan American Club

This is a summary of an 18-month contract for the Japan American Club, a medium-size, in-house school with schools in several cities.

Salary: ¥250,000/month.

Hours: 8 hours/day, 5 days/week. Teaching hours per day: 5 hours maximum. These times subject to change weekly according to the instructor's schedule, training and/or meetings. Hours may be split, with morning and evening hours and afternoons off.

Health Insurance: Company and employee share cost of accident insurance. Employee is responsible for health insurance

Housing: Company arranges for an apartment. Company pays key money and deposits; employee pays ¥20,000 damage deposit, which will be returned less damages and cleaning costs. Employee is responsible for rent, approximately ¥48,000 to ¥56,000. Company provides amenities such as stove, heater, futon, pots and pans, etc. The school has a phone rental plan.

Vacation: 5 days in May and August; 12 days in December.

Sick Leave: 5 sick days.

Bonus: Company pays for a one-way ticket to Japan.

Small School

The following is a summary of the provisions of a compensation package offered by a small in-house school that employs two teachers.

Salary: ¥250,000 month.

Hours: 30 hours a week.

Health Insurance: Employee pays own insurance.

Housing: School pays key money. Employee pays rent.

Transportation Expenses: Reimbursed.

Vacation: 1 week summer, 2 weeks winter, all national holidays.

Bonus: Pays air fare home.

Large, Multi-Branch In-Company School

These are the highlights of a large multi-branch school's compensation package. The contract itself is two legal-size pages in small print.

Salary: Guaranteed salary ¥250,000, except August and December, when employee will receive 75% pay (school closes one week each of those months). School will pay a higher salary to employees who provide documentation indicating a higher experience level.

Hours: 20 hours teaching a week. Employee must be available for teaching assignments Monday through Friday 9 a.m. to 9 p.m. Hours taught over 20 will be compensated in addition to guaranteed salary. Testing assignments and travel time in excess of 1 hour will be compensated separately.

Health Insurance: Company provides private health insurance.

Housing: School pays key money and deposits for employees stationed ouside of Tokyo.

Transportation Expenses: School reimburses for transportation expenses from employee's apartment to client company.

Vacation: All national holidays paid. One week in August and December, not paid. 3 days paid vacation after 6 months.

Bonus: ¥120,000 completion bonus at the end of contract.

Other Benefits: Free Japanese lessons.

Large In-Company School Contract of Employment

Following is a verbatim reproduction of the contract for a multi-branch in-company school.

Duration: The term of this contract is from 11/19/93 to 11/18/94, inclusive.

Termination of Contract: The employer may terminate this contract by giving thirty days written notification to Employee. Employee may terminate this contract by giving thirty days written notification to employer. In the event employee has borrowed monies from any parties in Japan under the sponsorship of employer, all such borrowed monies or debts must be paid in full upon notification of termination. Employer is authorized to deduct this amount from any monies due employee. Employer may take legal action for any damage caused by employee due to breach of contract.

Compensation: Employee will be paid each calendar month of work on the tenth day of the following month according to the following pay schedule:

Hourly rate: Daytime classes—¥3,000; Evening classes—¥3,500.

Compensation is based upon documented educational degrees/certificates and employment experience as submitted to employer by employee. If employee submits further documentation establishing a higher experience grade after the employment period commences, payment of the higher rate will be made from the first day of the following month after the documents have been presented to employer.

Employer guarantees that employee will be paid no less than ¥250,000 (gross wages) during every calendar month in which the employee is available for work assignments during all regular working days of the month. Employee agrees that whenever his/her availability is reduced, this guaranteed monthly income amount will be reduced for each day that employee is unavailable for work. This reduction will be proportionally equivalent to the ratio of working days missed to the total working days in that month.

Employer agrees to provide employee with a bonus of ¥120,000 upon satisfactory completion of the full duration of this contract.

Professional responsibilities: Employee agrees to: 1) fulfill the professional services expected of his/her position; 2) be available for work assignments Monday through Friday inclusive, from 8:00 a.m. to 9:00 p.m.; 3) attend orientations, training sessions and teachers' meetings as required by employer; 4) prepare adequately for each work assignment; 5) represent the employer to its clients in such a way as to satisfy the Employer/client contractual obligations; 6) adhere to the policies, rules and regulations of employer; 7) accept assignments outside the normal working days and hours if he/she has not been assigned enough work hours to earn the guaranteed minimum wages during any particular month; and 8) submit all required reports to employer on time.

Personal Responsibilities: Employee agrees to 1) be responsible for all debts incurred by or on behalf of himself/herself; 2) be responsible for maintaining and returning all company teaching materials that s/he uses; 3) acquire national health insurance or otherwise assume responsibility for the financing of his/her own personal health care requirements.

Conflict of interest: Employee agrees not to engage in any activity which will in any way interfere with the performance of his/her duties set forth in this contract and agrees not to work for any other employer during the term of this contract without written consent of the employer.

Conduct: Employee agrees to abide by the laws and regulations of the Japanese Government and absolves employer and its clients from all legal and financial obligations which may result from his/her actions.

Small School Contract of Employment

The following is the actual contract of the small school.

The Period of the contract: 1 year.

Working hours: 30 hours a week.

Holidays: 2 days a week; National holidays of Japan; 1 week summer vacation; 2 weeks winter vacation.

Work: Teach English class; telephone lessons, interview students; attend parties.

Notice: on leaving, you must give two months notice.

English Conversation Schools in Japan

Following are three lists of English conversation schools in Japan. All of this information was taken directly from help wanted ads published in the Japan Times *from October 1991 through May 1993. All of the phone numbers and addresses were verified before publication, but numbers change and schools go out of business. I apologize for any numbers that are incorrect.*

The first list contains the large multi-branch schools and their phone numbers in various cities. Next is a prefecture by prefecture listing of schools (a prefecture is the Japanese equivalent of a state). The list starts with schools in Tokyo, followed by Yokohama (part of the Greater Tokyo Area) and Osaka (Japan's second major city). Following Osaka the names of prefectures appear in alphabetical order and are bolded. The names of prefectures are followed by "-ken," *which is how the Japanese refer to prefectures. Kyoto and Hokkaido are not prefectures, but are included in this list.*

Under the prefecture heading I have listed major cities. The cities appear in italics with the suffix "-shi," *which means "city." If schools appear directly under the prefecture heading this means they are probably not located in a major city that could be easily located on a map of Japan.*

If the area code is the same for the entire city, it appears next to the name of the city. When schools listed more than one phone number, either in the same ad or over a period of time, all of those numbers are included.

The last list is of schools and their addresses in Japan. All of these schools can be found in the phone list.

Inclusion on these lists is in no way an endorsement of these schools as employers. I strongly advise that you carefully evaluate all schools as potential employers.

Multi-Branch Schools

The following are the large multi-branch schools. I have listed the school and then the phone number for the various branch offices. Each school will be listed again in the prefecture listing that follows.

AEON

Toll Free 0120/000-603
Tokyo 03/3359-5900
Gumma 0273/27-3663
Ibaraki 0292/24-3999
Kanazawa 0762/32-0785
Kobe 078/333-7773
Nagano 0262/26-1400
Nagoya 052/451-4300
Niigata 025/243-0440
Okayama 086/224-1200
Saitama 048/642-1666
Sendai 022/224-2727
Shizuoka 054/255-2608
Tochigi 0286/21-4018

Berlitz

Tokyo 03/3584-4211
03/3589-3525
Osaka 06/341-2531
Chiba 043/224-4151
Fukuoka 092/751-7561
Hiroshima 082/245-1521
Kobe 078/221-9371
Kyoto 075/255-2311
Nagoya 052/561-4611
Saitama 048/643-4671
Sapporo 011/221-4701
Shizuoka 054/273-2221
Yokohama 045/316-0261

Bilingual

Toll Free 0120/22-8191
Tokyo 03/3505-2844
Osaka 06/372-0805

Geos

Tokyo 03/5434-0200
Osaka 06/245-0032
Akita 0188/31-3117
Aomori 0177/77-2585
Fukuoka 092/725-5056
Kochi 0888/22-0064
Matsuyama 0899/43-3587
Morioka 0196/25-8850
Okinawa 098/868-3838
Sapporo 011/241-2066
Takamatsu 0878/33-3772
Tokushima 0886/25-4291

Interac

Tokyo 03/3234-7841
Fukuoka 092/473-6550
Hiroshima 082/240-7751
Nagoya 052/961-1031
Yokohama 045/681-7771

NOVA

Toll Free 0120/32-4929
Tokyo 03/5351-5601
Osaka 06/374-2622
Kyoto 075/252-0921
Yokohama 045/325-0300

Plady

Tokyo 03/3574-7231
Yokohama 045/316-4502

TCLC

Tokyo 03/3486-7667
Osaka 06/375-0287
Kita-Kyushu 093/522-6001
Nagoya 052/242-5939
052/262-7851
Mito 0294/36-7508

Schools Listed by Prefecture (ken)

This list begins with Tokyo, Yokohama and Osaka, the cities with the greatest number of schools. The rest of the list is in alphabetical order.

Tokyo (03)

A&S 3487-2293
Active Language 3587-6781
AEON 3359-5200
Shibuya 5489-5960
Ikebukuro 3983-0900
AIT 3700-8110
ALC Press 3323-3045
American School 3557-6851
American Express 3220-6100
ASA Staff Center 3320-8649
BEC 3352-2973
Berkeley House 3262-2710
Berlitz 3589-3525
Bilingual 3505-2844
Borgnan 3982-6651
CMS 3709-5961
Cosmopolitan 3273-7878
Days English School . . 5479-6756
Dobun Gaikokugo 3427-2220
ECC 3209-3884
ELEC 3265-8911
English House 3383-8008
English Studio 3712-3365
English Village 3779-2408
ETC 3924-3853
Excel Int'l. 5704-0311
Excellence Corp. 3234-4309
Gakken Gem Int'l 3476-3939
Gakken White House . 3495-6666
Geos 5434-0200
ICP 3463-5332
ICS 3239-0423
IEC 3619-0109
IES 5388-6030
3463-5396
Intec 3479-4861
Interac 3234-7841
Interlang 3497-5451
Interlink 3588-0022
JAL Academy 3477-2911
Japan Concept 5423-0531
Jiyugaoka Lang 3718-3511
Kamamoto English . . . 3341-6351
Kawamura Int'l. 3565-0292
Ken Lang. 3205-1230
Kent Gilbert Lang. 3478-8600
Kirby Gakuin 3342-6001
Lado Int'l. College 3366-7511
Lang. Instructors Guild 3355-4471
Liberty Int'l. 3821-1578
L.A. City College 3375-2345
Lin A 5486-9400
Marubeni 3234-1324
NCB 3346-8231
NCN 3593-1746
Nicholai Gakuin 3291-9254
NK Management Ctr. . 3217-2882
Nova 5272-8763
Ohtemachi Service 3273-2243
OTC 3552-8816
PACC 3353-7230
Pacific Lang. 3304-5098
Plady 3574-7231
PREP 5485-8686
Prime Academy 3271-0631
Sankei Int'l. College . . . 3760-4711
Selnate 5256-2601
Shinwa 3884-5916
Sony Lang. Labs 3504-1356
Sun Life 3367-4881
TCLC 3486-7667
3486-7634
Tess Lang. 3442-0125
Thomas English Inst. . . 3355-1621
TIE 3981-0591

TLI 3984-9281
Tokyo Jido Gakuin . . . 3447-4182
Tokyo Tech. College . . 3360-8832
Trendy House 3496-0903
Trinity Academy 3356-9144
Yamada Lang. 3323-7888
YMCA 3203-0171
3293-1921
Yomiuri Bunka Ctr. . . . 3292-4663

Yokohama (045)

America World 546-4664
Cecil School 314-8352
Cosmos 321-2621
Franks English 681-2266
Grow International 664-9036
Hitachi 861-0680
Interac 681-7771
Japan Grobic Co. 316-4119
S&S 331-3301
YCC American Club . . . 314-3911
YMCA 662-3721

Osaka (06)

American Village 367-0628
Berlitz 341-2531
Bilingual 372-0805
COS Language 386-9223
ECC 373-0144
English Workshop 571-4710
ESO 245-4919
FLS 314-1640
Geos 245-0032
ICP 241-0823
Ifu-Gaigo Gakuin 305-0721
KEC 347-7117
LL 868-3534
NCB 345-9111
NES 344-7701
Nova 374-2622
OTC 222-6125
Sony Language Labs . . . 372-6777
TCLC 375-0287
Toza 371-6460
Win 363-4462
World Gakuin 267-0032
YMCA 441-0892

Aichi-ken

Nagoya-shi (052)

ABC Academy 833-1982
AEON 451-4300
Berlitz 561-4611
Bilingual 561-7101
Forum 243-1100
GTC 562-1511
Interac 961-1031
Kent Gilbert School 541-1200
MALC 242-8491
Pencil English Center . . . 802-4156
Potato Club 323-5480
Sony Language Labs . . . 581-3371
TCLC 242-5939
Trident 735-1600
YMCA 331-6748

Chiba-ken

Excel Int'l. 0438/25-1545
Oxford 0438/22-0090
Sun Valley 0476/27-6796
YMCA (Kashiwa) . . 0471/45-3223

Chiba-shi (043)

ALS 422-0090
Berlitz 224-4151
Caring English School . . 273-8139
LSI 462-0388
Thames 277-9898
Top English School 254-5036
YMCA 279-8411

Funabashi-shi (0474)

IEC 71-7744
Shane 31-1220
YMCA 25-6366

Ehime-ken

Crossroads 0899/21-7595
Geos 0899/43-3587

Fukuoka-ken

Fukuoka-shi (092)

BBC 781-0341
Berlitz 751-7561
Geos 711-0482
Howdy English School . 592-5646
Interac 473-6550
Nova (Hakata) 412-3300
Seiha English School ... 733-6430
YMCA 831-1771

Kita-Kyushu (093)

Nova 531-1441
TCLC 522-6001
YMCA 511-0912

Fukushima-ken

ABC House 0246/54-6374
Nihonmatsu English 0243/23-0740
R&B English 0249/52-6822

Gumma-ken

YMCA 0272/34-2299

Hiroshima-ken

Hiroshima-shi (082)

Ace 211-1341
Berlitz 245-1521
Cosmo 211-1144
Interac 240-7751
Tomo Communications 223-7832
Will English School 248-6170
YMCA 228-2269

Hokkaido

CIE 0154/25-5227

Sapporo (011)

Berlitz 221-4701
EC Inc. 221-0279
Geos 241-2066
YMCA 561-5642

Hyogo-ken

Katayama 07914/3-3295
YMCA 0792/98-5566

Kobe (078)

AEON 333-7773
Berlitz 221-9371
Hawaii English 731-0650
TFI 221-2151
Time 411-0129

Ibaraki-ken

Ace 0298/22-1842
AEON 0292/24-3999
TCLC 0294/36-7508

Ishikawa-ken

Kanazawa (0762)

AEON 32-0785
Hokkoku Culture Center 60-3535
Sojusha 24-4900
YMCA 21-6748

Iwate-ken

YMCA 0196/23-1575

Kagawa

Eiken Institute 0877/63-3410
Geos 0888/22-0064
0886/25-4291
Language House .. 0878/34-3322
Lingo 0878/31-3241

Kanagawa-ken

AES 0462/24-3511
Babcock English ... 0463/94-2731
CBC 044/244-1959
Cranberry English . 044/733-8190
NSS.............. 0465/23-5381
Southern Cross Eng. 0467/54-1336

Fujisawa (0466)

Bear English Club 28-7090
Boston Academy 34-5947

KGC 26-0226

Kumamoto-ken

Kumamoto-shi (096)

Boston Academy 325-7974
IEC 535-5430
Washington Inst. 359-6083
YMCA 352-2344
353-6397

Kyoto

ACT 0774/20-3470

Kyoto-shi (075)

Berlitz 255-2311
NES 212-8110
Simul Academy 225-3100
YEA 221-8888
YMCA 231-4388

Mie-ken

Asahi Language ... 0592/24-4063
LACCO 0599/43-3030
YMCA 0593/53-3741

Miyagi-ken

Esther English Sch. 0229/23-5512

Sendai (022)

AEON 224-2127
LSI 384-5476
New Day 265-4288
Profit 266-8181
Sendai English Center .. 211-7171
Victoria Academy 276-3556
YMCA 222-7533

Miyazaki-ken

American Center .. 0985/53-4521
Pacific Lang Sch ... 0985/53-7824

Nagano-ken

A to Z Language .. 0266/23-0300
Apple Foreign Lang. 0263/33-1133
Suwa English 0266/58-3313

Nagano-shi (0262)

AEON 26-1400
Apple School 27-8587
English For You 23-1799
Let's 27-8800

Nagasaki-ken

YMCA 0958/22-5987

Nara-ken

American Bell Sch. . 07437/5-0515
Time 0742/27-5319
YMCA 0742/44-2207

Niigata-ken

Niigata-shi (025)

AEON 243-0440
Apple School 245-9339
Apple Foreign Language 223-4656
International Academy . 244-3161
Mashima International . 244-0155
NSG 244-1913
Wings 265-7257

Oita-ken

Cosmo English 0975/38-3188

Okayama-ken

Okayama-shi (086)

AEON 224-1200
Nova 227-2111
Okayama English Sch. .. 221-6070
Okayama Institute 231-5211
YMCA 223-1509

Okinawa-ken

YMCA 098/833-5904

Saitama-ken

ALEPH 0489/28-8100
Elm English 048/771-9591
New Life 048/756-5840
TYBIKS 048/736-5992
Ueno Gakuen 048/941-3121

YMCA 0484/76-3951
...................0429/39-5051

Omiya-shi (048)

AEON 642-1666
Berlitz 643-4671
Boston International ... 646-2535
Shogakukan Home Pal . 645-4961
YMCA 642-1521

Shiga-ken

Shiga English 0775/24-8879
YMCA 0748/33-2420

Shizuoka-ken

American Language 0559/22-6643
Every Language 0559/24-2818

Four Seasons 053/448-1501
Mills Academy 0559/48-2639
Universal English ..053/834-3647

Shizuoka-shi (054)

AEON 255-2608
Berlitz 273-2221
K&B 426-8996
Pioneer 426-0555

Tochigi-ken

Beavers 0284/72-3265
YMCA 0284/73-4373
0286/24-2546

Yamanashi-ken

Unitas English 0552/35-8335
YMCA 0552/35-8543

Addresses of English Schools in Japan

Most of these addresses were taken from advertisements found in the Japan Times. *A few I found from other places.Writing to schools and getting a response is really a gamble. But it's worth a try. Do you feel lucky?*

Tokyo/Yokohama

ACE Education Center
5-24-10 Sakai
Musahino-shi
Tokyo 180
Phone: 0422/52-0166

AEON
Shinjuku Gyoen Bld. 9F
2-3-10 Shinjuku
Shinjuku-ku
Tokyo 160
Phone: 03/3359-5900

AIT
3-20-1-401 Tamagawa
Setagaya-ku
Tokyo 158
Phone: 03/3700-8110

ALC Press, School Section
2-54-12 Eifuku
Suginami-ku
Tokyo 168
Phone: 03/3323-3045

American Express
Human Resources Dept.
4-30-16 Ogikubo
Suginami-ku
Tokyo 167
Phone: 03/3220-6100

Berlitz
Dai-ichi Kowa Bld. 5F
1-11-41 Akasaka
Minato-ku
Tokyo 107
Phone: 03/3589-3525

Inter School
Akasaka Yamakatsu Bld. 7F
8-5-32 Akasaka
Minato-ku
Tokyo 107
Phone: 03/3479-4861

Kawamura International Co.
Saeki Bld.
3-17-30 Shimo-ochiai
Shinjuku-ku
Tokyo 161
Phone: 03/3565-0292

Ken Language School
2-18-6 Yanagiya Bld. 5F
Takadanobaba
Shinjuku-ku
Tokyo 169
Phone: 03/3205-1230

Lado International College
Nishi Shinjuku Kimuraya 5F
7-5-25 Nishi Shinjuku
Shinjuku-ku
Tokyo 160
Phone: 03/3368-9278

Los Angeles City College
EPP Coordinator
1-53-1 Yoyogi
Shibuya-ku
Tokyo 151
Phone: 03/3375-2345

Sony Language Laboratories
4-2-11 Ginza
Chuo-ku
Tokyo 104
Phone: 03/3535-1260

Tokyo Jido Gakuin
KOA Bld.
1-19-10 Higashi Gotanda
Shinagawa-ku
Tokyo 141
Phone: 03/3447-4182

YMCA
7-1 Kanda Mitoshiro-cho
Chiyoda-ku
Tokyo 101
Phone: 03/3293-1921

YMCA Language Center
OSCY Coordinator
2-3-18 Nishi-Waseda
Shinjuku-ku
Tokyo 169
Phone: 03/3203-0171
Fax: 03/3207-0226

Grow International
Motomachi Plaza Bld. 1F
1-13 Motomachi
Naka-ku
Yokohama-shi
Kanagawa 231
Phone: 045/664-9036

Hitachi Keihin Inst.
850 Maioka-cho,
Totsuka-ku
Yokohama-shi
Kanagawa 244
Phone: 045/861-0680

YCC American Club
SY Bld. 6F
3-30-8 Tsuruya-cho
Kanagawa-ku
Yokohama-shi
Kanagawa 221
Phone: 045/314-3911

YMCA
1-7 Tokiwa-cho,
Naka-ku
Yokohama-shi
Kanagawa 231
Phone: 045/662-3721

Osaka

Ifu-Gaigo-Gakuin
3-3-4 Nishi-Nakajima
Yodogawa-ku
Osaka 532
Phone: 06/305-0721

LL School
Aikaiwa Bld.
2-1-28 Motomachi
Hattori
Toyonaka-shi
Osaka 561
Phone: 06/868-3534

Senri International School
4-4-16 Onohara-nishi
Mino-shi
Osaka 562
Phone: 0727/27-5050

World Gakuin
Dai-ni Yuraku Bld. 7F
4-1-7 Hon-machi
Chuo-ku
Osaka 541
Phone: 06/267-0032

YMCA
1-5-6 Tosabori
Nishi-ku
Osaka 550
Phone: 06/441-0892

Aichi-ken

Forum
Naka-Kuyakusho &
Asahi-Seimei Kyodo Bld. 13F
4-1-8 Sakae
Naka-ku
Nagoya-shi
Aichi 460
Phone: 052/243-1100

Pencil English School
Harashin Bld. 3F
1-515 Hara
Tempaku-ku
Nagoya-shi
Aichi 468
Phone: 052/802-4156

Sony Language Laboratory
Mainichi Bld. 5F
4-7-35 Meieki
Nakamura-ku
Nagoya-shi
Aichi 450
Phone: 052/581-3371

YMCA
2-5-29 Kami-maezu
Naka-ku
Nagoya-shi
Aichi 460
Phone: 052/331-6748

Chiba-ken

Excel
1-8-6 Yamato
Kisarazu-shi
Chiba 292
Phone: 0438/25-1545

YMCA
5-20-5 Masago
Chiba-shi
Chiba 280
Phone: 043/279-8411

Fukuoka-ken

Seiha English
2-1-14 Daimyo
Chuo-ku
Fukuoka-shi
Fukuoka 810
Phone: 092/733-6430

YMCA
2-3-9 Kajimachi
Kokura-kita-ku
Kita-kyushu-shi
Fukuoka 802
Phone: 093/511-0912

YMCA
1-1-10 Nankuma
Jonan-ku
Fukuoka-shi
Fukuoka 814
Phone: 092/831-1771

Fukushima-ken

Nihon-matsu English
1-90-2 Takeda
Nihon-matsu-shi
Fukushima 964
Phone: 0243/23-0740

Gumma-ken

YMCA
1-4-1 Kokuryo-cho
Maebashi-shi
Gumma 371
Phone: 0272/34-2299

Hiroshima-ken

ACE
Hakuho Bld. 5F
3-10 Hatchobori
Naka-ku
Hiroshima-shi
Hiroshima 730
Phone: 082/211-1341

Will English School
Princess Namiki Bld.
4-10 Mikawa-cho
Naka-ku
Hiroshima-shi
Hiroshima 730
Phone: 082/248-6170

YMCA
7-11 Hatchobori
Naka-ku
Hiroshima-shi
Hiroshima 730
Phone: 082/228-2266

Hokkaido

CIE
5-2 Nishiki-cho
Kushiro-shi
Hokkaido 085
Phone: 0154/25-5227

YMCA
11-2-5 Nishi
Minami 11-jo
Chuo-ku
Sapporo-shi
Hokkaido 064
Phone: 011/561-5642

Hyogo-ken (Kobe)

TFI Language School
Meijiseimi Bld. 6F
8-3-7 Isogami-dori
Chuo-ku
Kobe-shi
Hyogo 650
Phone: 078/221-2151

YMCA
2-7-15 Kano-cho
Chuo-ku
Kobe-shi
Hyogo 650
Phone: 078/241-7201

YMCA
9-15 Tsuchiyama
Higashinomachi
Himeji-shi
Hyogo 670
Phone: 0792/98-5566

Ishikawa-ken

Sojusha
Olympia Bld.
3-26 Oyama-cho
Kanazawa-shi
Ishikawa 920
Phone: 0762/24-4900

YMCA
44-1-201 Satomi-cho
Kanazawa-shi
Ishikawa 920
Phone: 0762/21-6748

Iwate-ken

YMCA
3-1-1 Hommachi-dori
Morioka-shi
Iwate 020
Phone: 0196/23-1575

Kagawa-ken

Language House
2-3-2 Kawara-machi
Takamatsu-shi
Kagawa 760
Phone: 0878/34-3322

Lingo School
11-6 Kamei-cho
Takamatsu-shi
Kagawa 760
Phone: 0878/31-3241

Kanagawa-ken

Southern Cross English
Akatsuki Kensetsu Dai-ni Bld. 3F
95-19 Kagawa
Chigasaki-shi
Kanagawa 253
Phone: 0467/54-1336

Kumamoto-ken

IEC
651-1 Hioki-machi
Yatsushiro-shi
Kumamoto 866
Phone: 0965/35-5430

YMCA
1-3-8 Shimmachi
Kumamoto-shi
Kumamoto 860
Phone: 096/353-6397

YMCA
Fukoku Seimei Bld. 8F
12-24 Hanabatake-cho
Kumamoto-shi
Kumamoto 860
Phone: 096/352-2344

Kyoto

Simul Academy
Karasuma Higashi-iru
Rokkaku-dori
Nakagyo-ku
Kyoto 604
Phone: 075/255-3100

YMCA
Yanaginobamba
Sanjo-dori
Nakagyo-ku
Kyoto 604
Phone: 075/231-4388

Mie-ken

YMCA
13-13 Nishi Shinchi
Yokkaichi-shi
Mie 510
Phone: 0593/53-3741

Miyagi-ken

New Day School
Yamaichi Kokubuncho Bld. 5F
2-15-16 Kokubuncho
Aoba-ku
Sendai-shi
Miyagi 980
Phone: 022/265-4288

Victoria Academy
1-5-15 Nankodai
Izumi-ku
Sendai-shi
Miyagi 980
Phone: 022/276-3556

YMCA
9-7 Tate-machi
Aoba-ku
Sendai-shi
Miyagi 980
Phone: 022/222-7533

Nagano-ken

A to Z Language
Via Apita Okaya 3F
1-1-5 Ginza
Okaya-shi
Nagano 394
Phone: 0266/23-0300

Apple Foreign Language
1-2-3 Fukashi
Matsumoto-shi
Nagano 390
Phone: 0263/33-1133

Apple School
1-3-8 Minami-chitose-cho
Nagano-shi
Nagano 380
Phone: 0262/27-8587

Let's
Wisteria 3F
1-8-1 Minami-chitose-cho
Nagano-shi
Nagano 380
Phone: 0262/27-8800

Nagasaki-ken

YMCA
1-4 Ofunaguromachi
Nagasaki-shi
Nagasaki 850
Phone: 0958/22-5987

Nara-ken

YMCA
2-14-1 Kunimi-cho
Saidaiji
Nara-shi
Nara 631
Phone: 0742/44-2207

Niigata-ken

International Academy
Priall Bandai 6F
1-1-32 Bandai
Niigata-shi
Niigata 950
Phone: 025/244-3161

Mashima International #209
1-2-3 Bandai
Niigata-shi
Niigata 950
Phone: 025/244-0155

Oita-ken

Cosmo English School
Mitsui Seimei Bld. 4F
2-9-24 Shuo-cho
Oita-shi
Oita 870
Phone: 0975/38-3188

Okayama-ken

AEON
2-3-23 Kosei-cho
Okayama-shi
Okayama 700
Phone: 086/224-1200

Okayama English School
Sanyo Bld. 2F
1-10-32 Omote-cho
Okayama-shi
Okayama 700
Phone: 086/221-6070

YMCA
1-5-25 Nakasange
Okayama-shi
Okayama 700
Phone: 0862/23-1509

Okinawa-ken

YMCA
2-17-3 Tsuboya-cho
Naha-shi
Okinawa 902
Phone: 098/833-5904

Saitama-ken

New Life English
1-3-28 Nishimachi
Iwatsuki-shi
Saitama 339
Phone: 048/756-5840

Ueno Gakuen College
2-3-1 Hara-cho
Soka-shi
Saitama 340
Phone: 048/941-3121

YMCA
Hasumi Bld.
1-46 Miyamachi
Omiya-shi
Saitama 330
Phone: 048/642-1521

YMCA
1-39-2 Kotesashi
Tokorozawa-shi
Saitama 359
Phone: 0429/39-5051

Shiga-ken

YMCA
537-3 Takakai-cho
Omi-Hachiman-shi
Shiga 523
Phone: 0748/33-2420

Shizuoka

American Language Service
1-10 Takashima-cho
Numazu-shi
Shizuoka 410
Phone: 0559/22-6643

Four Seasons
4-32-11 Sanarudai
Hamamatsu-shi
Shizuoka 432
Phone: 053/448-1501

Tochigi-ken

Beavers
257 Asakura-cho
Ashikaga-shi
Tochigi 326
Phone: 0284/72-3265

YMCA
2-7-42 Matsubara
Utsunomiya-shi
Tochigi 320
Phone: 0286/24-2546

Toyama-ken

YMCA
1-13-14 Tsutsumimachi-dori
Toyama-shi
Toyama 930
Phone: 0764/25-9001

Yamanashi-ken

YMCA
5-4-11 Chuo
Kofu-shi
Yamanashi 400
Phone: 0552/35-8543

Assistance via the Telephone

Except for the police and fire departments, all of the organizations listed below provide English-speaking operators to assist you.

Police and Emergency (probably not in English) 110

Fire and Ambulance (probably not in English) 119

Japan Travel Phone

Eastern Japan (Toll Free) 0120/222-800

Western Japan (Toll Free) 0120/444-800

Tokyo 03/3503-4400

Kyoto 075/371-5649

Tourist Information Centers (TIC)

Tokyo 03/3502-1461

Kyoto 075/371-5649

Narita Airport 0476/32-8711

Japan East Railways 03/3423-0111

NTT Phone Information

Tokyo 03/5295-1010

Narita 0476/28-1010

Yokohama 045/322-1010

Osaka 06/313-1010

Nagoya 052/541-1010

Kimi Information Center (in Tokyo) 03/3986-1604

U.S. Embassy (in Tokyo) 03/3224-5000

Canadian Embassy (in Tokyo) 03/3408-2101

British Embassy (in Tokyo) 03/3265-5511

Australian Embassy (in Tokyo) 03/5232-4111

Japanese Survival Phrases

Japanese is easy to pronounce. Just remember that a *is pronounced like* ah, e *like* eh, i *like* ee *in "feet,"* o *like* oa *in "moat," and* u *like* oo *in "coo." The doubling of an* o *or* u *or other vowel when a word is romanized doesn't change the sound of the vowel but doubles its length. Below, a hyphen is used to set off the different syllables that make up each word. Where you see* s(u) *it means the u is unvoiced (so the word ends in an* ess *sound).*

Basic Phrases

Hello	*Kon-ni-chi-wa*	こんにちは
Good morning	*O-ha-yo-*o *go-za-i-ma-s(u)*	おはよう ございます
Good evening	*Kon-ban wa*	こんばんは
Good-bye	*Sa-yo-o-na-ra*	さようなら
Excuse me	*Su-mi-ma-sen*	すみません
I am sorry	*Go-men-na-sa-i*	ごめんなさい
Thank you	*A-ri-ga-to-o*	ありがとう
Thank you (formal)	*Do-o-mo a-ri-ga-to-o go-za-i-ma-s(u)*	どうも ありがとう ございます
You're welcome	*Do-o i-ta-shi-ma-shi-te*	どう いたしまして
Just a moment, please	*Chot-to mat-te ku-da-sa-i*	ちょっと　まって ください

Asking for Help

Do you speak English?	*E-i-go o ha-na-shi-ma-s(u) ka?*	英語を 話しますか？
Do you understand?	*Wa-ka-ri-ma-s(u) ka?*	わかりますか？
I don't speak Japanese.	*Ni-hon-go wa wa-ka-ri-ma-sen.*	日本語は わかりません。
I don't understand.	*Wa-ka-ri-ma-sen.*	わかりません。

Where is (the) _____?	______ *wa do-ko de-s(u) ka?*	______ は どこですか？
police box	*ko-o-ban*	交番
toilet (restroom)	*to-i-re*	トイレ
telephone	*den-wa*	電話
this place	*ko-ko*	ここ
train station	*e-ki*	駅
subway	*chi-ka-te-tsu*	地下鉄
How much is the fare to _____?	_____ *ma-de i-ku-ra de-s(u) ka?*	_____ まで いくら　ですか？
What platform for _____?	_____ *yu-ki wa nan-ban sen de-s(u) ka?*	_______ 行は なんばん線 ですか？
Where does this train go?	*Ko-no den-sha wa do-ko ma-de?* (or simply point to the train and say, *Do-ko ma-de?*)	この電車は どこまで？
How much is this?	*Ko-re wa i-ku-ra de-s(u) ka?* (or just say, *I-ku-ra des(u) ka?*)	これは　いくら ですか？
Please give me ______.	______ *o kudasai.*	____をください。

Simple Directions

straight	*mas-su-gu*	まっすぐ
right	*mi-gi*	右
left	*hi-da-ri*	左
north	*ki-ta*	北
south	*mi-na-mi*	南
east	*hi-ga-shi*	東
west	*ni-shi*	西

Japanese Food Menu

This Japanese menu includes some of the more inexpensive items that will give you the nourishment you need to survive in Japan while you are waiting to find a job. I have provided the name of the food in English, followed by the Japanese translation and, where appropriate, a Japanese pronunciation aid.

Noodles

A quick and inexpensive meal is a bowl of noodles. You can find noodle shops everywhere. Train stations are a good place to look. Basically there are three types of noodles, but they can be served with many types of ingredients. It is cheaper to just order the basic noodle.

Udon うどん. White flour noodles served in a broth with *kamaboko* (a kind of pressed fishcake), onions, and sometimes other goodies.

Soba そば. Grayish buckwheat noodles served in a broth with *kamaboko* and other goodies.

Ramen ラーメン. Chinese noodles served in a broth with a slice of pork.

Don-buri

A *don-buri* どんぶり (丼) is a big bowl of rice served with cooked egg, sauce, and vegetables. Varieties include:

Oyako-don 親子どん. *Don-buri* with chicken.

Ten-don 天どん. *Don-buri* with shrimp *tempura*.

Gyu-don 牛どん. *Don-buri* with meat.

Katsu-don カツどん. *Don-buri* with pork cutlet.

Unagi-don うなぎどん. *Don-buri* with cooked eel.

Tempura 天ぷら. *Tempura* is fish, shrimp, and vegetables dipped in batter and deep fried. It usually comes with rice.

Curry rice カレーライス (*ka-ree ra-i-su*). Rice with curry sauce and some meat. Not as spicy as you would find in India, but it makes an inexpensive, filling meal.

Set Lunches

Many restaurants offer lunch deals like those I described on page 87. They are called either *teishoku* 定食 or *setto* セット.

Morning service モーニングサービス (*mo-o-nin-gu saa-bis[u]*). As described on page 88, look for coffee shops that offer these inexpensive breakfast sets.

Drinks

You can get all the drinks you're used to, but why pay for them when the green tea is served free?

Green tea お茶 (*o-cha*). Traditional Japanese tea, a bit bitter (but you never add sugar or milk).

Milk ミルク (*mi-ru-ku*). Not cheap. May take some getting used to.

Beer ビール (*bii-ru*). Not cheap, but very tasty.

Coffee コーヒー (*ko-o-hii*). Cheapest coffee is at the fast-food restaurants. Coffee in a coffee shop is pricy and strong.

Cola コーラ (*ko-o-ra*). If you need a soft drink, buy it from a vending machine.

At the Convenience Store

Japanese snacks at convenience stores like 7-11 can be an inexpensive way to hold you over to your big meal of the day. Some cheap things to look for include:

Onigiri おにぎり. Basically a ball of rice with a piece of fish or vegetable inside, all wrapped up in a crisp piece of seaweed.

Bento 弁当. *Bento* are like boxed lunches. Served cold, they include rice, fish, pickled vegetables, a piece of meat, potatoes, and various other things. Just look over the selections in their clear plastic containers and pick out one that looks good.

Crackers and chips. In Japan you don't find the same selection of snack foods you are used to at home, but be a little adventurous and try some. As at home, these foods don't offer much value for the money.

Index